The Pocket Essential

JAMES CAMERON

First published in Great Brita

Pocket Essentials, 18 Coleswo   ; AL5 1EQ

Distributed in the USA by Trafalgar Square Publishing, PO Box 257,
Howe Hill Road, North Pomfret, Vermont 05053

Copyright © Brian J Robb 2002
Series Editor: Paul Duncan

A CIP catalogue record for this book is available from the British Library.

ISBN 1-903047-95-1

2 4 6 8 10 9 7 5 3 1

Book typeset by Wordsmith Solutions Ltd
Printed and bound by Cox & Wyman

There's no one else a book on James Cameron could be dedicated to but my son, Cameron James Colin Robb.

Acknowledgements

The works of Marc Shapiro, Christopher Heard and Paula Parisi were invaluable route maps through the work and life of James Cameron. Also, those online archivists and collectors of Cameron-related cuttings and trivia (too many to mention) deserve thanks...

CONTENTS

1. James Cameron: King Of The World?

"When I get to the end of a film, fifty per cent of my crew usually believes I'm a complete asshole. The other fifty per cent *knows* I'm a complete asshole!"

– James Cameron

James Cameron, director of *Titanic, Terminator 2* and *Aliens*, infamously dubbed himself "King of the world" at the 1998 Oscar ceremony. Cameron had reached his professional peak as *Titanic* claimed 11 of those sought-after golden statuettes.

At the time Cameron was married to actress Linda Hamilton (who'd starred in his two *Terminator* movies). He'd been through two marriages already (to producer Gale Ann Hurd and director Kathryn Bigelow). After *Titanic*, he divorced Hamilton (with whom he had a daughter) to marry *Titanic* actress Suzy Amis and have another child with her. As unsettled as he was in his private life, so has James Cameron been unsettled in his professional film-making career.

As far as movie critics are concerned there are two James Camerons. There's the director who did more than almost any other through the formulaic high-concept years of the 1980s and 1990s to layer his movies with a degree of human interest, with characters who appear to have lives, loves and concerns beyond the boundaries of each individual film. Alternatively, Cameron is the director who did more than any other to bury these same characters, stories that seem to matter and any signs of humanity beneath a deluge of special effects and artifice.

Those working on any James Cameron film would recognise the idea that there are two versions of the director, but they might put it in different terms. There's "Jim," the personable, sometimes charmingly boyish director as excited by making his films as he hopes audiences will be when they see them. It's Jim who strives to do fantastic work every time, who pushes his cast and crew to get the best from them, who wants everything to be perfect. Then there's 'Mij,' the evil alter ego of James Cameron, identified by those who have worked with him, particularly on *True Lies*. It is Mij who drives his cast and crew mad with take after take in search of that elusive perfection. It is Mij who takes every movie he makes and turns it into an overblown blockbuster which also busts studio budgets. It's Mij who risks life and limb (not always his own) in making his movies. And it's Mij who goes through his relationships like there's no tomorrow...

Cameron has an audience waiting to see his movies. He has known that since the unexpected, amazing success of *The Terminator*. He has never been happy, though, to churn out the same old film. Even in his sequels (to his own *The Terminator* or to Ridley Scott's *Alien*) he has been determined to take things in a different direction.

It's in search of the new and different that Cameron has pursued innovation in film after film. From breakthroughs in special effects (*Terminator 2: Judgment Day*) to breakthroughs in simple spending (*True Lies, Titanic*), Cameron has always been pushing forward. Along the way he has made enemies (most of the studios who employed him have seen executives meet with the wrath of Mij) and been caricatured by the press as an out-of-control megalomaniac. Somewhere inside mild-mannered Jim is shouty-and-huffy Mij just waiting to burst out. James Cameron knows he needs both sides of his personality – the writer of human interest stories and the creator of astounding special effects – to successfully pull off his movies and to connect with his audience.

Titanic, the film which finally made everything good in Hollywood for James Cameron, was the culmination of everything he knows about filmmaking and his definite career high point. Attempting to balance personal stories (those of Sarah Connor in *The Terminator*, Ripley in *Aliens*, Bud Brigman and his ex-wife Lindsey in *The Abyss*, Harry Tasker and his wife in *True Lies*, Jack and Rose in *Titanic*) with epic stories and events (nothing less than the future of mankind in the *Terminator* movies, the survival of man against the aliens, the fate of the world (again!) in *The Abyss*, a terrorist plot in *True Lies* and the sinking of the *Titanic*) has been Cameron's self-appointed task. He has always reached high and fallen low (especially in *True Lies*) as a result, but finally hit pay dirt with the doomed romance of *Titanic*. Here he reached beyond the SF fans and male teen audiences drawn to the worlds of the *Terminator*, *Aliens* or even Harry Tasker (*True Lies*). *Titanic* reached a widespread mainstream audience, from male and female teenagers (drawn by Leonardo DiCaprio and Kate Winslet and the tragic romance of it all) to pensioners, who saw in *Titanic* a gloriously old-fashioned epic film brought to life using the latest in computer graphics technology.

In fact, James Cameron is a product of the Hollywood way of making movies. Everything must be bigger and better than the last hit movie and hang the expense (as long as there's a percentage return!)... It's a tough business with high stakes and no one ever enjoys success in Hollywood by being nice. That's how James Cameron gets away with unleashing Mij, whether it be on studio executives complaining that his latest film is over schedule and way over budget, or on cast and crew members who are not as driven as he is to achieve that elusive movie perfection.

It's only because James Cameron delivers the goods that he continues to get away with it. With worldwide grosses of $157 million (against a budget of $18 million) on *Aliens*, over $100 million (against a budget of $41 million) on *The Abyss*, almost $500 million on *Terminator 2* (against a $90 million budget), over $360 million on *True Lies* (against a budget of $95 million, and that's considered a flop!) and (the true biggie) over $1.3 billion for *Titanic* (against that infamous $200 million budget), James Cameron looks set to continue to 'get away with it' for some time to come...

2. The Spawning

Childhood And Formative Influences

The town of Kapuskasing in Ontario, Canada, is never going to trouble the history books. Its one claim to fame is of the Hollywood variety: *Titanic* film-maker James Cameron was born there on 16 August 1954.

Growing up, Cameron was torn between the examples of his disciplinarian electrical engineer father Phillip, who worked at the local paper mill, and his independently-minded artist mother Shirley, who would encourage her son to explore his creative side. In the end, he inherited Shirley's artistic temperament crossed with his father's workaholic attention to detail. Neither of his parents suffered fools gladly.

By 1959, when James Cameron was five, the family had followed Phillip Cameron's employment to Chippewa, near Niagara Falls. It was the first of several moves that would bring Cameron to Hollywood. Before he got there, Hollywood made its mark on him when, at the age of 15, he saw Stanley Kubrick's *2001: A Space Odyssey*. The story of a manned space mission sent to explore a mysterious anomaly near Jupiter, the film captured the imagination of Cameron in a way that few others had before. Specifically, it was the dramatic and majestic special effects sequences of Kubrick's drama which got the 15-year-old thinking. "I just couldn't figure out how all those visual effects were done," admitted Cameron, looking back. "I wanted badly to know, to understand what I was seeing. I went back to see the movie 10 times, trying to get inside it." It's significant that it was the visual effects, not the story, not the characters or the sense of mystery that captured James Cameron's adolescent attention.

Cameron, along with his younger brother Mike, had always been a tinkerer, building his own catapults and go-carts and even a submarine which, according to a Cameron myth, claimed the lives of several mice when he launched it over Niagara Falls. Living most of his childhood next to various bodies of water was to have a profound effect. "When you grow up listening to hundreds of thousands of gallons of water thundering in the distance, this constant roar, it's like growing up next to the ocean," he told *Maclean's* magazine. "It just becomes part of your being."

Inspired by the Kubrick movie, Cameron lay his hands on a second-hand 16mm movie camera. It was the first step towards a career that would not only change his life but change American movies.

Imitating *2001*, Cameron began constructing model spaceships to film. Lacking any real technical knowledge, the wannabe film-maker embarked on a trial-and-error process. He would see what worked and what didn't, what looked good and what looked fake, figuring out how much he could get away with in faking convincing cinematic images. This learning process would stand him in good stead when he later began working for Roger Corman.

The thought of actually working in the movie business seemed unreal to James Cameron as he attended High School in Ontario, Canada. "For me, the idea of being a film-maker was completely innocent," he told *Current Biography*. "I had a fascination with it, but in all honesty, I couldn't see myself as a film director. After all, film directors came from Hollywood, not from Niagara Falls." However, another change of job for Phillip Cameron in 1971 brought the family to Orange County, south of Los Angeles in California, US. If there was one thing that Cameron knew about Los Angeles, California, it was that it was home to Hollywood, which was in turn home to movie-making.

Aged 18 and located in California in 1972, James Cameron was actually no closer to working in the film industry. With five children to look after, his parents couldn't afford for him to attend film school, so Cameron found himself enrolled at Fullerton College where he started studying physics. He discovered physics was merely maths in disguise and nothing to do with outer space, so quickly switched to English literature. Cameron was, not for the first time, torn between the disciplines of his parents. "I didn't know whether I wanted to be a scientist or an artist..."

During this time Cameron was distracted from his goal of a Hollywood career by real life, rather than 'reel life.' Having dropped out of college in 1976, Cameron moved into a small, suburban tract house with local Orange County waitress Sharon Williams, whom he'd been seeing for around five years. James Cameron's day job was driving a truck or, occasionally, the local school bus. Yet the Hollywood ambition lay dormant within him.

In the summer of 1977, James Cameron's world changed again when he went to see a new movie called *Star Wars*. "I was really upset when I saw *Star Wars*," admitted Cameron, recalling *2001* and his own crude film-making experiments. "That was the movie that I wanted to make. After seeing that movie I got very determined. I decided to get busy."

11

Xenon Genesis (1977)

AKA *Xenogenesis*

Crew: Director: James Cameron; Writers: James Cameron, William Wisher Jr.

Cast: Margaret Undiel (Laurie), William Wisher Jr. (Raj)

Plot: Two humans are searching space for a place where the cycle of creation can begin again.

Inspiration: Returning to his film-making ambitions after the experience of *Star Wars*, James Cameron put all ideas of pursuing any other career out of his mind. He'd taught himself a great deal about making movies through his 8mm and 16mm experiments and through reading every book on film-making in the library of the University of Southern California in Los Angeles. Now was the time to put all that into practice.

Cameron found himself involved with a group of Southern Californian dentists from nearby Tustin, California, who were looking to fund a movie as a way of sheltering some of their money from tax. Here was his chance. From a list of 10 movie outlines Cameron had written with his friend William Wisher and submitted to these weekend movie moguls, they chose *Xenon Genesis*, an idea Cameron described as "an alien special effects movie."

Production: Planned as a full-length feature film, budgeted at a mere $400,000, *Xenon Genesis* was rapidly rethought as a 12-minute showcase short when the dentists could only provide $20,000 in funding. That didn't matter to Cameron. Here was a chance to try his hand a making a 'real' film without putting any of his own money on the line. "They wanted me to do *Star Wars*, of course," Cameron told *Omni* magazine in 1989. "They didn't want to spend that kind of money. I was game. I had nothing to lose..."

Friends, including co-writer Wisher and girlfriend Sharon Williams, were roped into the project, decked out in spacesuits made of tinfoil and paraded around Fullerton College's eye clinic, which served as the film's principal location.

Cameron scoured model shops in the area, buying up plastic model kits of battleships and aeroplanes, then scratch-building model spaceships for his film, just as he'd done for his earlier private 8mm efforts.

While he knew what he was doing in getting the special effects on screen, Cameron was not as confident when it came to directing actors, even if they were amateurs and friends. "On the first day of shooting I found myself with $40,000 of rented camera equipment and no idea how to use any of it," admitted Cameron. "We had to figure it out the hard way..."

One of the first shots in the can for *Xenon Genesis* was a glass matte shot, combining a real landscape with a painting-on-glass for a cheap in-camera effect. "That worked out real fine," claimed Cameron.

His financiers were not as confident. Four months into production the dentists began to have second thoughts about sheltering their spare funds in movie production. Funding dried up and production on *Xenon Genesis* ground to a halt. The result was little more than a glorified home movie. "I hesitate to think what kind of film I might have made at that point in my development as a film-maker," said Cameron of his first attempt to make a real movie.

The end of the production was marked by the marriage between Sharon Williams and James Cameron. Sharon had supported Cameron when he was out of work by pulling extra waitressing shifts and had tolerated his movie-making madness for over five years. Although she may have thought getting married was her reward for her patience and forbearance, it wasn't long before Cameron was back at work on his celluloid dreams. Not wanting to waste the work on *Xenon Genesis*, Cameron cut together what he had into a 12-minute 35mm promotional reel. "It was crudely edited," Cameron told *Film Comment* in 1985, "but there was a visual narrative there and the special effects were pretty good..." In fact, *Xenon Genesis* was good enough to act as a calling card that would land James Cameron his first real job in Hollywood.

Battle Beyond The Stars (1980)

Crew: Director: Jimmy T Murakami; Writers: John Sayles (script), Anne Dyer (story); Producers: Ed Carlin, Roger Corman, Mary Ann Fisher; Original music: James Horner; Cinematography: Daniel Lacambre; Film Editing: RJ Kizer; Art Direction: Charles Breen, James Cameron; Costume Design: Dorinda Rice Wood; Visual Effects: James Cameron (miniature constructor)

Cast: Richard Thomas (Shad), Robert Vaughn (Gelt), John Saxon (Sador), George Peppard (Cowboy), Darlanne Fluegel (Nanelia), Sybil Danning (Saint-Exmin), Sam Jaffe (Dr Hephaestus), Jeff Corey (Zed)

Plot: The Magnificent Seven in space. Seven futuristic mercenaries are assembled to defend a helpless farm colony from an evil overlord.

Inspiration: It has always seemed ironic that for a film-maker who would pride himself on his budget-busting reputation James Cameron started off his film-making career working for Roger Corman. Corman, from the 1960s to the 1990s, was America's pre-eminent low-budget exploitation film-maker. Cameron wasn't alone in cutting his teeth at the Corman film factory. Among other alumni of the cheap and cheerful Corman method were accomplished film directors like Martin Scorsese, Francis Ford Coppola, Joe Dante, Jonathan Demme, Peter Bogdanovich and Ron Howard.

For Cameron the Corman experience was to be incredibly significant. Like Corman himself, who'd begun his film-making career in the mail room of 20th Century-Fox in 1949, Cameron was willing to start at the bottom of the film-making ladder and work his way to the top.

In the wake of the success of *Star Wars* in 1977, film-makers the world over began producing their own swashbuckling space epics in the hope of riding George Lucas' wave of success. From Italy's *StarCrash* to Corman's *Battle Beyond The Stars*, the late 1970s saw a glut of cheap and sometimes not-so-cheerful sci-fi flicks. Corman had been here before, producing knock-off movies to capitalise on the latest film trend, whether it be juvenile delinquent pictures, dinosaur movies or gothic horror creepies.

Aware that Corman was preparing a *Star Wars* knock-off movie, James Cameron came calling at Corman's Venice, LA, studio with his 12-minute *Xenon Genesis* compilation, ready to show it to anyone who'd see him. Cameron was met by the head of Corman's special effects department, Chuck Kaminsky. Impressed by Cameron's work, Kaminsky had to break the news that there were no vacancies for special effects cameramen. However, he could offer the very confident Cameron a job as a model builder in the special effects department.

That was enough for Cameron. "I wasn't talking 'director,'" Cameron told *US Magazine* in 1991 of his first visit to Corman's movie factory. "I was saying, 'I can build miniatures, I can work an effects camera, I know a little about animation.' I wasn't looking for anything more..." Readily accepting the job, Cameron reckoned he was on his way to Hollywood greatness. "I figured I would get in there and spread like a virus," he told *Premiere* magazine in 1994. "It was the best possible place for me..."

Production: Battle Beyond The Stars was – at $2 million rather than his usual $500,000 – a 'big-budget' Corman production. Aiming to cash in on the *Star Wars* mania, Corman had assembled a better than usual cast with George Peppard and Robert Vaughn leading this *Seven Samurai* in space tale. The script was by John Sayles (*The Brother From Another Planet*) and the director was Jimmy T Murakami (*When The Wind Blows*).

"In 1980, Roger was doing the most expensive film he'd ever made, *Battle Beyond The Stars*. I got sucked into that vortex. It was totally out of control," Cameron told *Omni* in 1989. "This was a film where nobody knew what was going on. Nobody in Corman's outfit had ever made a film remotely that size. They didn't understand visual effects. It was complete chaos." That chaos worked to Cameron's advantage: "I found I did pretty well in a chaotic environment. I could manipulate the situation to position myself to a) learn what I needed to learn, b) do what I wanted to do, and c) advance to the next level. If they gave me the credits I should have on that picture, I would have five or six. I did matte paintings, was a visual effects cameraman, ran my own visual effects motion control unit, designed and built three-quarters of the sets as art director. I was a model builder and designed and built a front projection system. I operated it on the first day of shooting, then turned it over to some other people and went on to be the art director. I was skipping from one job to another."

Cameron thrived and was soon making himself indispensable. As production began, the hero's spaceship had not been designed. This was a job Cameron quickly volunteered for, as much because it would bring him into contact with Corman as for the opportunity to work on something practical. "It was a totally goofy design," Cameron told *US Magazine* of his first effort. "It was a spaceship with tits."

It was good enough for Corman, though, and Cameron found himself working on many more miniatures for the movie. Matching the miniature work with the live action footage was proving to be a problem and it was Cameron who came up with a solution, in the form of a series of matte paintings and a front projection system which would put the actors believably into the imaginary locations of the film. As a result, Cameron found himself in charge of the newly-created Corman process projection and visual effects department.

While impressing Corman by saving money and time, Cameron was not impressing some of his colleagues. In fact, this young man in a hurry was quickly gathering something of a reputation as an arrogant and cruel worker. Asserting his new-found authority on the film, Cameron fired the art director and merged the art department with his own, taking on both jobs. Just the year before, he'd been messing around in Fullerton, shooting never-to-be-seen footage with friends. Now he saw his chance to make his mark and there was no way he was going to miss out, even if that meant rubbing some people up the wrong way. As long as Corman was happy and the film got made on time and on budget, that was all that mattered. "I had only been there a month and all of a sudden I was head of this department. Everybody else who worked there really hated me," admitted Cameron, "and I don't blame them..."

The workload meant that Cameron wasn't spending much time in Orange County with wife Sharon. To avoid commuting and to be closer to the Corman studio, Cameron rented an apartment in Venice. He asked Sharon to move up with him but she refused to leave family and friends behind. It was the beginning of the end of their marriage. "I came to the realisation that Jim wasn't married to me anymore," Sharon told *The National Enquirer*, "he was married to his work."

As a result, Cameron threw himself even more into his work on *Battle Beyond The Stars*. "Jim functioned as model builder, effects cameraman and art director all on the same shot," marvelled Corman, who thought he'd seen it all in his many years making next-to-no-budget epics.

"Thanks to *Battle Beyond The Stars*, Roger had inadvertently built a visual effects facility. He had motion control cameras, all this junk lying around, and these stages... and then the movie was over. Everybody had their noses to the grindstone. A week or so before *Battle* ended, it occurred to me that we were all going to be out of a job. But there was this opportunity. At a party, I met Joe Alves, Spielberg's production designer on *Jaws*. Joe was working with [director] John Carpenter; they were looking for a visual effects facility. I said come on down to the facility. I'll bet we can underbid everybody. We're hungry, we've got nothing else to do, the place'll be empty in a week. I was selling Roger's place, and Roger didn't even know about it."

Analysis: Although impressive if considered as a film from the no-budget Roger Corman stable, *Battle Beyond The Stars* is essentially a rather dull retelling of the *Seven Samurai/The Magnificent Seven* story. John Sayles (who later went on to greater things as an independent film-maker) provided an occasionally witty script, which was well realised by James Cameron's special effects, model work and sets. The whole is let down, though, by Murakami's stodgy direction and Corman's own sausage line production style. So impressed was Corman by the effects work, supervised by Cameron, that he recycled them wholesale in his 1983 film *Space Raiders* (this time capitalising on *Raiders Of The Lost Ark*... in space!)

Escape From New York (1981)

Crew: Director: John Carpenter; Writers: John Carpenter, Nick Castle; Producers: Barry Bernardi (associate producer), Larry J Franco (producer), Debra Hill (producer); Original music: John Carpenter, Claudio Simonetti (Italian version); Cinematography: Dean Cundey, Jim Lucas; Film Editing: Todd C Ramsay; Production Design: Joe Alves; Costume Design: Stephen Loomis; Visual Effects: Stephen Barncard (motion control design), James Cameron (matte artist)

Cast: Kurt Russell (Snake Plissken), Lee Van Cleef (Bob Hauk), Ernest Borgnine (Cabbie), Donald Pleasance (President of the United States), Isaac Hayes (The Duke of New York), Season Hubley (Girl in Chock Full O'Nuts), Harry Dean Stanton (Brain/Harold Helman), Adrienne Barbeau (Maggie)

Plot: 1997. A plane carrying the US President crash-lands on Manhattan Island, a sealed-off maximum security prison. Only one man can rescue him: war veteran Snake Plissken.

Inspiration: James Cameron met production designer Joe Alves while working on *Battle Beyond The Stars*. Alves was in pre-production on another science fiction feature film, John Carpenter's *Escape From New York*. He was having budget problems, though, as all the effects houses he was dealing with for the film were proving to be too expensive. Never one to miss a trick, Cameron invited Alves for a guided tour of Corman's New World Studios facility. Alves brought Carpenter and [producer] Debra Hill. They had 25 shots that needed to be done for *Escape From New York*. "We just smoothed right in. Suddenly Roger had a viable enterprise on the side that he could keep alive using other people's money until he needed it again. We ended up underbidding just about every other effects house in town," said Cameron. "Of course after we got the job we had to turn around and figure out how to do it for that amount of money."

Production: Wrapping production on *Battle Beyond The Stars*, which had proved to be a baptism of fire for Cameron, the young would-be film-maker immediately began work on the pre-production of *Escape From New York* the very next day.

Unlike *Battle*, this job was to be a smoother ride. "[It was] the most relaxed project to ever go through New World," claimed Cameron in an interview with *Fangoria* magazine. "We were able to do a lot of planning and storyboarding, everything was produced according to a flow chart. Everything was completed on time and within budget."

Falling back on the process camera he'd developed for *Battle*, Cameron was able to deliver some technically convincing model work for Carpenter's very tight budget. One sequence in particular shows Cameron's touch: Plissken pilots a hang-glider over the walls of Manhattan to land on top of the World Trade Centre.

Cameron was bringing the Corman approach to bear on non-Corman projects, and it would be an approach that would inform all of his later filmmaking endeavours, no matter how large the budget. "I got a lot of good experience working for Roger. What I learned was 'Just go for it...' I learned there was always a way to get it done and make it presentable. Roger's kind of low-budget mentality teaches you that you can probably get by with a lot less than you think..."

Analysis: Introducing the character of Snake Plissken (who'd return in *Escape From LA*), Carpenter's movie is a showcase for Cameron's early low-budget effects work. The glider landing and some of the miniatures make a significant contribution to creating the world in which Carpenter's film takes place.

Galaxy Of Terror (1981)

AKA *Mindwarp: An Infinity Of Terror (1981), Planet Of Horrors (1981)*

Crew: Director: Bruce D Clark; Writers: Bruce D Clark, Marc Siegler; Producers: Roger Corman (producer), Mary Ann Fisher (producer); Original music: Barry Schrader; Cinematography: Jacques Haitkin; Film Editing: Larry Bock, RJ Kizer, Barry Zetlin; Production Design: James Cameron; Art Direction: Steve Graziani, Alex Hajdu; Set Decoration: Bill Paxton, KC Scheibel; Costume Design: Timaree McCormick

Cast: Edward Albert (Cabren), Erin Moran (Alluma), Ray Walston (Kore), Bernard Behrens (Ilvar), Zalman King (Baelon), Robert Englund (Ranger), Grace Zabriskie (Trantor)

Plot: Alien meets *Solaris* but on a non-existent budget. Responding to an SOS, the crew of a spaceship explore a planet where their every subconscious fear and terror become reality.

Inspiration: Seeing the chance to further his career again and to work on another science fiction movie following *Battle* and *Escape*, James Cameron lobbied Roger Corman to take on the role of production designer on *Galaxy Of Terror*, Corman's *Alien* clone.

"The timing was perfect: We were just finishing *Escape From New York*, and Roger was getting ready to go on to his next science fiction film, *Galaxy Of Terror*," Cameron noted in a 1986 *Omni* interview.

As with his contribution to *Battle Beyond The Stars*, Cameron found his willingness to take on further roles resulted in him becoming art director and, more importantly, second unit director on the film. That meant he could get behind the camera and direct, not just model shooting but live action actors. It would only be one more step from here to directing a film for Roger Corman and the completion of the master plan which had formed in Cameron's mind when he'd first crossed the threshold of New World Pictures.

"I think that [*Galaxy Of Terror*] was] the one that showed the most cohesive design and execution of effects," claimed Cameron, while still acknowledging that the film was far inferior to the original *Alien* movie. "We didn't even use any *Battle Beyond The Stars* footage on that one," he said, referring to the Corman habit of recycling old footage – especially effects footage created by Cameron – in new films.

Production: Much of *Galaxy Of Terror* featured the main characters wielding space ray guns, which Cameron quickly set about designing. His cheap Corman solution was to acquire some real guns and wrap them in a suitably high-tech fibreglass outer case. This was a great, low-budget solution to create working guns, until producer Aaron Lipstadt pointed out to Cameron that to use the guns, "We had to have a licensed armourer on set every time. I had to tell Jim that we couldn't afford this guy to come out every time these guns were working, which was every day... He thought it would be cool to use these guns, and he was really angry that we couldn't use them."

During the 30-day shoot on *Galaxy Of Terror*, Cameron found himself coming up against all sorts of seemingly insurmountable challenges, only to overcome them and move on. One particular sequence involved a character's arm covered with wriggling maggots. Naturally, Cameron had a fake arm and a box of earthworms to work with. "The worms were supposed to be wriggling around over the arm," said Cameron. "But they just sat there..." His solution was to wire the prop up for electricity. Calling 'Action,' he flipped the switch to turn the power on. "The worms started moving like crazy. Then I said, 'Okay, that's good. Cut.'" This scene was witnessed by two visiting Italian film producers. The Corman studio was regarded as a hotbed of new talent so there were often visitors to the set. Cameron had been too busy working to take note of these newcomers. They, however, were taken aback by what they saw. "The worms stopped moving. I turned around and these two producers are standing there, gaping."

The producers took their opportunity. After a quick chat, James Cameron found he'd taken another step forward in his Hollywood ambitions. "I guess they figured that if I could get a performance out of maggots, I should be okay with actors. So they offered me their film." James Cameron had just agreed to direct his first movie, *Piranha II*.

Analysis: Another step on in the master plan for Cameron, but one that showed he was rapidly running out of reasons to stay at the Corman film factory. As so often with Corman, the production values and special effects are well done, but the script and the acting let the whole thing down.

Trivia: Galaxy Of Terror features an intriguing cast who all went on to 'better' things: Erin Moran was in *Buck Rogers In The 25th Century* on TV, Ray Walston was *My Favourite Martian*, Robert Englund found infamy as phantom killer Freddy Krueger in the *A Nightmare On Elm Street* series, while Zalman King enjoyed his own kind of infamy as the creator of soft porn TV series *The Red Shoe Diaries* and films like *9½ Weeks*. Incidentally, the cinematographer was Jacques Haitkin, who went on to fulfil the same role on Wes Craven's *A Nightmare On Elm Street*.

Piranha II: The Spawning (1981)

"I can honestly say that *Piranha II* is the best flying piranha movie ever made."

– James Cameron

AKA *Piranha II: Flying Killers (1981), Piranha Part Two: The Spawning (1981), Piranha paura (1981) (Italy), The Spawning (1981) (USA)*

Crew: Directors: James Cameron, Ovidio G Assonitis (uncredited); Writer: HA Milton; Producers: Ovidio G Assonitis (executive producer), Chako van Leeuwen (producer), Jeff Schechtman (producer); Original music: Stelvio Cipriani; Cinematography: Roberto D'Ettorre Piazzolli; Film Editing: Roberto Silvi; Production Design: Vincenzo Medusa, Stefano Paltrinieri; Costume Design: Nicoletta Ercole

Cast: Tricia O'Neil (Anne Kimbrough), Steve Marachuk (Tyler Sherman, Biochemist), Lance Henriksen (Steve Kimbrough, St Anns Police Dept.), Ricky Paull Goldin (Chris Kimbrough, credited as Ricky G Paull), Ted Richert (Raoul, Hotel Manager), Leslie Graves (Allison Dumont), Carole Davis (Jai), Connie Lynn Hadden (Loretta)

Plot: Jaws with wings. The inhabitants of a Caribbean island are terrorised by a host of mutated flying piranha fish, the result of a government experiment gone wrong.

Inspiration: Joe Dante's *Piranha* (1978) was an unashamed Roger Corman-produced low-budget rip-off of Steven Spielberg's *Jaws*. Despite the disparity between the two movies, *Piranha* nevertheless found an audience who enjoyed the witty, rough-and-ready feel to the film. Decent reviews and good box office meant that a sequel seemed inevitable. Corman, however, wasn't convinced and he sold the sequel rights, as part of a distribution deal with Warner Brothers, to Italian producer Ovidio G Assonitis.

Assonitis, impressed by then 25-year-old James Cameron's ability to electro-shock a performance from a maggot, tapped him to direct *Piranha II: The Spawning.* Cameron would later discover that he'd been hired merely to fulfil a contractual obligation to Warner Brothers for a US-based director and cast, but at the time he simply saw an opportunity to direct a movie.

Cameron was no fool and knew that the project was likely to be a thankless task, but it was an opportunity not to be overlooked. "I knew it would be tremendously difficult," he told *Fangoria.* "It was an ambitious project with very little money and it was being shot out of the country [in Jamaica]. I wouldn't have access to all the people I normally would have approached. I would end up having to supervise an entire crew that spoke only Italian..."

Production: "I was warned by a lot of people that *Piranha II* would be a bad experience," noted Cameron, who'd heard that producer Ovidio G Assonitis could be hands-on and interfering, "but it looked like a shot, so I took it."

Arriving in Jamaica in February 1981, after a self-taught crash course in Italian, Cameron found himself caught up in a situation he hadn't anticipated. Expecting to begin pre-production and to be able to make his mark on the initial, rather poor, script by HA Milton, Cameron discovered that pre-production was well underway. Not only had hundreds of sketches, production drawings and storyboards already been completed by the Italian crew, but the majority of the work was "just abominable," according to Cameron. "The producer tried to convince me to stay and fix things in the remaining three weeks of pre-production. At the same time I was rewriting the script. Like a moron, I agreed."

Knowing he was working with less-than-great material, Cameron nevertheless tried to structure the story so that dramatically it made sense and allowed for some degree of character development. While he wrote the revised screenplay, the director was also hand-building and painting the mutant fish of the title after rejecting the rubber props presented to him by the Italian special effects team.

Just before shooting started the cast, including Lance Henriksen, Tricia O'Neil and Ricky Paull arrived to discover that the budget did not stretch to providing costumes for their characters and they'd have to wear their own clothes. Having taken the job simply for the salary, actor Lance Henriksen found himself allayed with director Cameron against the Italian producer. "Jim really wanted to make this movie," recalled Henriksen. The night before shooting a scene requiring Henriksen to wear a military-style uniform, the pair were discussing the problem over dinner. "[Jim] turned and spotted a waiter who was wearing a uniform that was real close to what we needed. He immediately went up to the waiter and bought the uniform with his own money."

With no money for costumes, there was no money for stuntmen, either. Cameron relied on persuading the actors themselves to undertake any stunt-work required, which included Lance Henriksen jumping from a helicopter to the sea. In the process, the actor injured his hand, which continued to trouble him for the remainder of the shoot.

Having been assured by Ovidio G Assonitis that the film would not be a 'porno shoot,' the producer informed Cameron that he'd be shooting some extra scenes he'd written for the film on the other side of the island. Cameron thought little of this development, even when he found out that the Assonitis scenes involved topless women. Still thinking he had final cut on the film, he felt confident he could just omit whatever unsuitable material Assonitis shot.

Twelve days into shooting on *Piranha II*, James Cameron was called into Assonitis' office in Jamaica and fired from the film. "This wacko producer just fired me," Cameron told *Maclean's* magazine in 1997. "He took over directing the film. I thought I was doing a good job, but he told me everything was shit and that nothing cut together."

Cameron had become suspicious when Assonitis refused to let the director see the 'dailies,' the previous day's footage which has been printed up. Assonitis began to drop hints that the material Cameron was shooting was not going to cut together, while Cameron told the producer he'd need to see the footage to understand what additional material had to be shot to make the scenes work.

He didn't get the chance. "Hiring me and then firing me is what he had in mind the whole time," Cameron said of Assonitis' plan to get around the requirement for an American director on the project. The producer went on to complete the shoot and cut the movie.

Cameron was willing to put *Piranha II* down as a learning experience and leave it at that, until he discovered that the film would still be released with his name attached as director. He had returned to Los Angeles in March 1981, but he then followed Assonitis to Rome where the producer was editing the film. There he offered to help edit the movie, but Assonitis wouldn't let the director have final cut. Staying in a hotel room, running out of money and eating room service leftovers from trays dumped outside other people's rooms for collection, Cameron decided to embark on a campaign of stealth editing on *Piranha II*. At night he'd break into the editing suite and work on his own cut of the film. "I went through all the footage and saw that, yes, there was a movie there, but unfortunately they weren't cutting it that way." This progressed until Assonitis figured out what was going on and had the by now seriously ill director removed.

Returning to California, Cameron offered Warner Brothers his services to recut the film for American release. They agreed and the result is the widely available 95-minute cut of the movie. Far from perfect, it at least makes sense... after a fashion.

Like most B-movies, *Piranha II* opened to indifference, but managed to make its costs back. "I don't feel it was my first picture," James Cameron told *US* magazine. "I decided to use it as a credit when it would do me some good and to drop it when it would not do any good. I think that makes sense. There is no truth but what we make."

Rep Company: Lance Henriksen (spelt Henricksen on the credits) has the honour of becoming the first member of the James Cameron regularly reused rep company, although he surely wants to forget all about *Piranha II*.

Reception: 'This is a routine monster film with an idiotic premise and laughably phoney special effects.' – *Variety*. 'You would have to be psychic to have spotted any talent from James Cameron in this picture.' – *Leonard Maltin*. 'It is a production that outdazzles its gratuitous, violent counterparts.' – *The Hollywood Reporter*

Analysis: Sure, it's a knock-off of a *Jaws* knock-off (and not a terribly good one at that), but at the centre of *Piranha II* is the work of a film-maker who knew he must be destined for better and bigger things. The script is terrible, the acting awful (with the glaring exception of Lance Henriksen, who does himself proud in the circumstances as a latecomer to acting) but *Piranha II* has been crafted with more attention to detail and more care than you'd perhaps expect. It's the work of a director taking an opportunity (however limited) laid before him to practise his nascent craft.

Indeed, scratching the surface, it's possible to discern within *Piranha II* some themes which would later emerge through the body of James Cameron's work. For example, the underwater photography and the way the undersea wreckage is shot surpass most low-budget films of this time and stand out within the film as the work of a director with more interest in making a quality film than the producers or the script deserve. Through *The Abyss* to *Titanic* and his documentary *Ghosts Of The Abyss*, the world of wrecked ships located under the sea recurs again and again through Cameron's work.

Then we have the marital relationship of Anne Kimbrough (Tricia O'Neil) and Steve Kimbrough (Lance Henriksen). They're married but apart and have a son. Anne enjoys a brief fling with Tyler Sherman (Steve Marachuk), the biochemist investigating the Government and military creating flying killers, while the situation on the island serves to eventually bring husband and wife back together. It's a plot structure that would echo through *The Abyss*, while romances of one type or another lie at the heart of *True Lies* and *Titanic*. Even putting Anne Kimbrough at the centre of the action would later be followed by Cameron's self-created female protagonists of *Aliens* and *Terminator 2: Judgment Day*. Although he's not credited, Cameron did heavily rework the script and has clearly used some of the structure, characters and obsessions he'd later feature in other work which he did control.

The piranha attacks are brief but effective, with Cameron cleverly hiding his monsters as much as possible, but happily (and again, effectively) showing the results of the attacks. Even the limited T&A material shot and inserted by the producer doesn't detract too much from the overall competency of Cameron's professional debut.

Trivia: In a classic piece of dialogue, Tyler Sherman asks Anne of her cop husband: "You know that robot?" Of course, Lance Henriksen, playing Anne's husband, would go on to play the android Bishop in James Cameron's *Aliens*! Was Cameron thinking ahead?

The Verdict: 1/5

3. Tech Noir

The Terminator (1984)

"I feared failure when I was making *Terminator*. I was worried about whether or not I was a film-maker at that point..."

– James Cameron

Crew: Director: James Cameron; Writers: James Cameron & Gale Ann Hurd, Harlan Ellison (source screenplays *Soldier* and *Demon With A Glass Hand*, originally uncredited), William Wisher Jr. (additional dialogue, as William Wisher); Producer: John Daly (executive producer), Derek Gibson (executive producer), Gale Ann Hurd (producer); Original music: Brad Fiedel, Tane McClure (songs, uncredited); Cinematography: Adam Greenberg; Film Editing: Mark Goldblatt; Art Direction: George Costello; Set Decoration: Maria Rebman Caso; Costume Design: Hilary Wright

Cast: Arnold Schwarzenegger (The Terminator, T-800), Michael Biehn (Kyle Reese), Linda Hamilton (Sarah Connor), Paul Winfield (Detective Lieutenant Ed Traxler LAPD), Lance Henriksen (Detective Vukovich LAPD), Rick Rossovich (Matt Buchannan, Ginger's Boyfriend), Bess Motta (Ginger Ventura, Sarah's Room-Mate), Earl Boen (Dr Silberman, Police Criminal Psychologist), Dick Miller (Pawn Shop Clerk), Shawn Schepps (Nancy), Bruce M Kerner (Central Division Desk Sergeant), Franco Columbus (Future Terminator), Bill Paxton (Punk Leader, Spikey Blue Hair), Brad Rearden (Punk), Brian Thompson (Punk), William Wisher Jr. (Policeman)

Plot: An organic cyborg killing machine in human shape is sent back in time from war-ravaged 2029 to LA in 1984, to find and eliminate Sarah Connor, the mother of the military leader battling the dominant machine intelligence in the future.

Inspiration: The Terminator sprang from a dream... While alone in Rome battling to save his first directorial effort, *Piranha II*, James Cameron fell ill. Living in a hotel in a city where he didn't speak the language, sneaking into the editing room trying to 'save' his movie and surviving on leftover scraps from other guests' room service meals, Cameron fell victim to a particularly virulent flu bug.

In his fever dreams he saw visions, images of skeletal men arising from flame. "I would see these images of a metallic death figure rising Phoenix-like out of fire," he told *Maclean's* magazine. "I woke up and grabbed a pencil and paper and started writing..." From Cameron's alienation came the character which was to make his name in Hollywood. "I was surrounded by people I could not get help from," Cameron recalled of his experience in Rome in *Premiere* magazine. "I felt very alienated and so it was easy for me to imagine a machine with a gun. At that point of the greatest alienation in my life, it was easy to create the character [of the Terminator]."

Development: Cameron returned to Los Angeles in mid-1981, a changed man from the gung-ho film-maker who'd set off to battle his Italian producer and rescue his debut directorial effort. *Piranha II* had provided experience for Cameron, good and bad, and he was now determined to make use of that experience to gain a foothold in Hollywood. Perhaps his first movie wasn't great, but Cameron knew he was capable of producing something much better, given half a chance.

The door at Roger Corman's New World was open for him to return, but the prospect of handling low-budget special effects or even becoming a director for hire on C-movie productions did not appeal. "I knew I was never going to be offered another movie unless I came up with something myself," Cameron claimed to *US* magazine. "I had to write a film that made sense to me as a director. I had to not price myself out of the kind of budget that studios were likely to trust me with."

For Cameron that meant writing his own project, a prospect which had never appealed to the very visual director. He'd come to film-making through the special effects and art direction route, not through the creation of characters and story. His work had always been in service to screenplays created by others. Perhaps that explains why Cameron's first original screenplay for *The Terminator* borrowed so liberally from the work of others as well as comic books, myths and legends. Later the director would admit that his inspirations were two Harlan Ellison episodes of the SF TV series *The Outer Limits (Soldier* and *Demon With A Glass Hand)*, comic books of the 1980s like Frank Miller's *The Dark Knight Returns* and the legend of Siegfried and his quest for a magical weapon.

Despite his reluctance to write, Cameron found he'd gathered enough source material, combined with his nightmarish vision from his trip to Rome, to allow him to knock out a first draft screenplay very quickly. A 45-page manuscript was the result, but many months of work, research and thought were required to turn this basic outline into a practical screenplay for the purposes of film-making.

While Cameron and his old friend Bill Wisher worked on developing the screenplay, the would-be director realised he had to do something quickly to make some money. The result was a return to New World studios as a 'design consultant' on Aaron Lipstadt's movie *Android* (1982). The two-week job saw Cameron come into the production department to contribute design ideas during the pre-production stage of the movie. It was enough to bring in some ready cash to allow him to complete the full screenplay of *The Terminator*. Presenting the project to an agent who'd agreed to represent Cameron on the back of *Piranha II*, he was told the movie was a "lousy idea." Cameron's response was to fire his agent.

"Roger [Corman] always attributes [a film's failure] to the poster being wrong or the title being wrong," recalled Cameron. "He knows that his films aren't in the market long enough for word of mouth to be a factor. If the title and poster are working, he's selling tickets. I remembered the lesson of the Corman-style campaign which had nothing to do with the movie. A year or so later, having written *The Terminator*, waiting, waiting, waiting to get that picture started, I was starving and had to take some work. I worked as an illustrator doing posters for movies that were pure and utter cheese. They were so bad that most of them were direct to video. I couldn't watch them, they were so bad. They were for a couple of very small independent releasing companies that I think are now out of business. They paid pretty well. I could knock out a one-sheet painting in a day, day and a half and make a couple of grand for it. At my subsistence level lifestyle at the time, I could live for two months on that. I'd work for two days and write for two months. I couldn't watch the films, so I'd just make up anything. I'd just riff on the titles. There was some horrible karate movie, and I did a *Road Warrior* thing of one guy kicking another off a motorcycle. There was no scene like that in the movie."

During early 1982 he continued to work with Bill Wisher on the screenplay of *The Terminator*. Wisher worked, in particular, on some of the early character stuff with Sarah Connor and some of the police station scenes. Gale Ann Hurd, whom Cameron had met when they were both toiling away at New World, shared Cameron's passion for the developing script and felt it certainly had potential. "When the script was completed [in May 1982]," she told *Starlog* magazine, "we were convinced that we had all the ingredients for a successful movie."

Several major studios agreed when Hurd touted the project around town. She now owned the rights to the project, having paid Cameron $1 for them, on the proviso that if the film went into production he would direct and

27

she'd produce. However, those studios who were interested in the project wanted to buy the script, not the team of Hurd and Cameron. Some studios attempted to persuade Hurd to agree to produce but cut loose Cameron as director. She refused. "The more we heard, 'This is a great project but we want a real producer and a real director to do it,' the more convinced we were that we had something good," noted Hurd.

"I wasn't interested in dealing with the studios because I knew that as a director I had no chops," Cameron told *Omni* magazine. "If I sold the [*Terminator*] script to Paramount, for instance, I knew what the deal would be: They would agree to do 'best effort' to let me direct the film, but [when] push came to shove I'd be bumped aside. That was a given. If I had a script that people wanted, and I kept my claws sunk into it, I had a good shot at directing it if I stayed in low-budget independent world."

Working their way down the Hollywood food chain, Cameron and Hurd secured a meeting with John Daly of Hemdale, who were interested in finding out more about the project. In a gimmicky attempt to make an impact, Cameron had *Piranha II* actor Lance Henriksen dress as the Terminator character and visit Daly immediately before Cameron and Hurd. It was this touch of showmanship, as much as the script itself, which was to find the screenplay a home.

Production: James Cameron wanted a budget of $8 million to make his movie, but the Hemdale deal only offered him $4 million. Undaunted, the director proceeded to make his movie as if he were making an $8 million project. Casting was the first order of business, and Cameron found his suggestions of Michael Biehn or Lance Henriksen as the title character shot down. In the early versions of the screenplay, the Terminator character was described as an 'everyman,' someone who would not look out of place on a modern city street, not the larger-than-life figure Arnold Schwarzenegger would later play. Hemdale's deal involved distributor Orion Pictures in the production of *The Terminator*. Their representative, Mike Medavoy, wanted ex-American football star OJ Simpson to play the title character, with muscleman Schwarzenegger suggested as the hero-from-the-future Kyle Reese. Simpson was eventually rejected, ironically – given subsequent events in his life – as his 'good guy' image was a hindrance to him playing the role. Cameron, who was considering German actor Jurgen Prochnow for the title role, was left with Schwarzenegger. Schwarzenegger had read the screenplay and claimed no interest in playing Reese (an idea Cameron hated), but privately was attracted by the role that he felt might have more impact, that of the Terminator itself. Cameron set out for a meeting with Schwarzenegger aiming to pick a fight with the actor by suggesting he play the villain instead of the hero, thereby forcing him off the picture. To their surprise, both actor and director came away from the meeting with a new direction: Schwarzenegger would play the Terminator. "Once Arnold was cast, the complexion of the picture changed completely," recalled Cameron. That casting allowed Cameron to put Michael Biehn, his pal from the Corman days, in the role of the heroic Reese.

"It turned out that there weren't that many viable stars who could be cast as those characters [the Terminator and Reese]. Arnold Schwarzenegger's name came up via Orion, who had some money in the picture. Hemdale had an output deal with them. Arnold was proposed as the good guy. And OJ Simpson was proposed as the killer! We never considered that a viable possibility," confirmed Cameron in an *Omni* interview. "The Arnold thing I knew wasn't going to go away, at least not until I met Arnold. Plus, I wanted to meet him. I thought he was cool, [although] I knew that Arnold was not right for Reese. Reese was a very verbal character, a guy who's just rapping off information. Arnold didn't strike me as a guy who could deal with page after page of dialogue at that time. He can do it now hands down; we've proven that. He essentially plays the Reese character in *Terminator 2*. Arnold is 'Irving the Explainer' in the second film, [just as] Reese was in the first one."

The trickiest piece of casting was to be that of the heroine, Sarah Connor, the target of the Terminator, mother of the future resistance leader John Connor and love interest for Kyle Reese. It was a difficult role to fill because it was a very demanding part in a film which didn't have a huge budget to hire top flight acting talent. A search for an actress who was unknown, therefore affordable, but seemed to have what it would take to bring the character to convincing life and hold the screen against Schwarzenegger and Biehn, led Cameron to Linda Hamilton. Hamilton had featured in *Children Of The Corn* and several other low-budget movies, but she seemed to Cameron to capture both the vulnerability of Sarah and the inner steel which would be required as the character faced up to her fate. Additionally, Cameron cast Lance Henriksen, his original choice for the lead character, as doomed cop Vukovich.

"That was a tough call on my part," said Cameron about downgrading Henriksen from would-be Terminator to run-of-the-mill cop role. "Lance was a friend. At a certain point I shared [*Terminator*] with him 'cause we were friends. He got excited about it. I actually saw him playing the Terminator, because we'd always made the assumption that the Terminator would be an unknown actor. He was supposed to be this anonymous face in the crowd that could walk up and kill you."

Cameron had definite reasons for wanting the Terminator to be more like an ordinary guy. "My idea at that time was he showed up as a blank slate and had to draw from everybody he met," recalled the director. "That didn't really pay off so much in the first film, although there is the scene where he takes the mother's voice. It really pays off in the second film. Then you realise that both characters are about mimicry. I took that to the logical extreme with the T-1000 [*T2*'s evil robot], where he could not only pick up vocal mannerisms but the whole physical aspect of someone."

With the casting finally in place, production of *The Terminator* came to a grinding halt when it became clear that Schwarzenegger's previous contractual obligations to the producers of the *Conan The Barbarian* series of movies meant he would not be available to shoot on the project for some time. Cameron turned the delay to good use. His screenplay for *The Terminator* had won him some scripting offers which he was now in a position to accept. Despite his constant denials that he wasn't a writer and that writing the screenplay was continually the hardest part of any project for him, he found himself tapped to turn out screenplays for two high-profile sequels: *Rambo, First Blood: Part 2* (1985) and *Aliens* (1986). As writer for hire on the *Rambo* sequel, Cameron had to contend with the involvement of the film's star, Sylvester Stallone, in the writing process, while for the *Aliens* sequel the only guidance he was given by producers Walter Hill and David Giler was: "Ripley and soldiers." Simultaneously, Cameron would work on *Rambo, Aliens* and revisions and developments on his *Terminator* script, aiming to clear all three before the start date on *The Terminator* in early spring 1984.

Before that, Cameron had to take care of some personal business. Although now living with production partner Gale Ann Hurd in a small house in Tarzana, about 20 miles outside of LA, James Cameron was still married to his wife Sharon. Their divorce was little more than a formality. Cameron didn't want a reconciliation, but Sharon did, although she was willing to settle the divorce with a payment of just $1,200. "She thought [film-making] was just a passing hobby," Cameron told *The Los Angeles Times* in 1986. "I'm convinced that getting into film professionally is what killed that marriage. It was a different world for her and she just couldn't go with it..." The first of James Cameron's marriages had come to an end.

As Schwarzenegger trained for his role physically and in weapons handling, Cameron hired Stan Winston to realise the film's special effects.

Winston was wary of working with a director who'd been so involved in special effects previously, but the concept and opportunity of the movie won him over. "There was already a concept that was quite brilliant," said Winston, "and I didn't want to change it." Just before production began, in March 1984, Cameron's leading lady chipped her ankle bone and was almost replaced. It was only due to Cameron's loyalty to Linda Hamilton as his first choice that she was retained. Now he could finally shoot those images which had haunted his dreams for years: "This movie has all the things in it I wanted to see in a movie when I was 16: robots, pretty girls, time travel and action!"

Shooting on *The Terminator* was a 10-week process, with eight weeks of night filming because so much of the movie took place after dark. Shooting took place largely in and around Los Angeles after Toronto was rejected as a possible venue. Cameron set out to project an image of control during shooting, even though inside he was nervous about his ability to achieve what he'd set out to put on film. "It was a real rush to direct the film," he would later tell genre magazine *Starlog*, "but there was a great deal of terror involved as well... I feared failure when I was making *Terminator*. I was worried about whether or not I was a film-maker at that point..."

Detail-oriented, Cameron impressed most of his cast with his attention to the minutiae of the process, especially Arnold Schwarzenegger who was taken aback by Cameron's knowledge of film-making techniques, if not by his way of dealing with actors. Schwarzenegger found himself being directed in intimate detail, down to when to move and what direction to look in. Cameron had good reason for taking this approach: "Arnold was still learning about being an actor and since I was the director, he did what I told him."

Shooting progressed smoothly, especially through a week of pyrotechnic work for the attack on the police station during which many actors had to wear exploding squibs, which simulated being hit by bullets. "Jim was using these big explosives which went off like shotgun shells," recalled Lance Henriksen of the sequence. "Actors were getting real burns from the force of the blasts." That wasn't enough to stop Cameron, setting a pattern for his future film productions where his actors were not considered by him to be real people, but simply elements needed to bring his filmic vision to cinematic life.

As production wore on, especially during the night shooting, dissent began to arise. Linda Hamilton, in particular, had trouble working with her demanding director. "Jim was a taskmaster," she told *The Los Angeles Vil-*

lage View. "He didn't make a lot of room to satisfy his actors. He had a reputation for not treating people very well and that's exactly what happened to me..."

The special effects required to bring the title character to life were especially demanding, but here Cameron was in his element. Alongside Stan Winston, the director used every trick in the book, from indistinct lighting, stop motion animation, puppetry, special make-up effects and model work to bring his Terminator, the "ultimate robot in the ultimate robot movie" to the screen. One model shot – an out-of-control tanker crashing and exploding – took three months to prepare and then went hideously wrong on the one and only take possible, The whole sequence had to be remounted and filmed successfully within seven days.

Principal photography wrapped in June 1984 and the film went straight into post-production, allowing no let-up for James Cameron. Cameron's final cut of the film ran to 103 minutes, with only a further two minutes removed to make a tight action picture out of the miles of footage he'd shot. Having been left alone by studio executives during pre-production and photography, in an echo of his *Piranha II* experience, Cameron suddenly found himself butting heads during the editing process. Hemdale chairman John Daly was adamant that the film should end with the explosion of the oil tanker. Cameron, however, didn't feel this was an adequate wrap-up to the wider story the movie was telling. He won out, but the fight was to lead to bigger problems with Hemdale and Orion.

Fearing that the film they'd produced was set to die at the box office, Orion decided not to put much money or effort behind promoting the film, with ads running only in the week before release and a poster based around a bare-chested Schwarzenegger was produced in an attempt to pull in a female audience as well as the action-loving males. Cameron was furious that his movie, described by the studio a "a down-and-dirty little action thriller that would last three weeks in theatres" was "being treated like dogshit." Cameron, however would have the last laugh, because the film was released to fantastic reviews and surprising box office.

Reception: 'A blazing cinematic comic book full of virtuoso film-making, solid performances and a compelling story.' – *Variety.* 'A cracking thriller full of all sorts of gory treats. The film is loaded with fuel-injected chase scenes, clever special effects and a sly humour.' – *The Los Angeles Times.* 'It is a B-movie with flair and, as directed by James Cameron, has suspense and personality.' – *The New York Times.* 'A near perfect example of the genre that will melt the hinges of your jaw.' – *Newsweek.* 'A feral crackerjack B-movie, roiling with noisy, body splattering shoot-outs and edited with Samurai fleetness.' – *The Village Voice*. 'A perfectly enjoyable barrage of science fiction and mayhem.' – *The Los Angeles Weekly*

Box Office: The Terminator became the US number one box-office movie for three weeks running following its mid-October 1984 opening. The opening weekend of 26 October 1984 saw the film take $4 million in ticket sales. The film ran into December still drawing big box-office numbers, but enjoyed no more advertising or promotional support from Orion. Despite that, *The Terminator* went on to outperform two of that season's big SF movies which were expected to be hits: *Dune* and *2010: Odyssey Two*. Costing only $6.4 million, nicely midway between Hemdale's original budget of $4 million and Cameron's desired amount of $8 million, the film went on to gross almost $40 million in the US, with an additional $35 million from overseas. James Cameron had arrived on the Hollywood directorial A-list.

Rep Company: Take a good look at one of the punks who the Terminator fights at the beginning of the movie. The one who gets thrown against the gate is none other than soon-to-be Cameron regular Bill Paxton (a long way from *Titanic*). Lance Henriksen reappears as Detective Vukovich. Appearing for the first time in a James Cameron film is Michael Biehn (who'd later co-star in *The Abyss*). Linda Hamilton would recreate Sarah Connor in *Terminator 2*, and Arnold Schwarzenegger would appear in *Terminator 2* and *True Lies*, directed by Cameron.

Analysis: "I was trying to make a movie about how we become inhuman, how society and technology can dehumanise the individual, whether it's a psychiatrist, police officer or soldier," said James Cameron of his ambitions with *The Terminator*. "All the various archetypes shown in both [*Terminator*] films are representatives of a dehumanising process of technology. *The Terminator* is not about something else; it's about us. It's about technology held up in the image of man. We did it to ourselves, that's the message. If this horror comes from the future in the form of a skull made of titanium, we created it. That's why it's in our image."

The Terminator introduces one of James Cameron's great themes: the stranger out of time. Reese and the Terminator itself fulfil this role, but it recurs in several of Cameron's movies: Sigourney Weaver's Ripley in *Aliens*, Ed Harris' oilman Bud Brigman in *The Abyss*, Sarah Connor herself in *Terminator 2*, Arnold Schwarzenegger's civil servant-cum-spy Harry Tasker in *True Lies*, both Jack and Rose in *Titanic* and even Max (Jessica Alba) in the TV series *Dark Angel*. Each character is out of time or out of place, just as Cameron was himself when stranded ill in Rome among people who didn't speak his language. It was in that mental space that he created *The Terminator* concept.

The obvious opposition in *The Terminator* is between the anti-life title character, more machine than man, and the pro-life (the father of the world's future saviour, John Connor) Kyle Reese. The T-800 is introduced as more than a man: physically imposing and (as seen in the opening barroom confrontation) invulnerable. Computerised point of view shots and Schwarzenegger's unusual speech rhythms are used to point up the character's inhumanity. Reese, meanwhile, is vulnerable, affected by the 'weaknesses' of humanity: yet, it is those very weaknesses (compassion, caritas, empathy, the ability to improvise, to think beyond his 'programming') that allow Reese and Sarah Connor to triumph over the machines, both in the present of the 1980s and in the future war.

Linda Hamilton was one of the first of the new 1980s breed of female action heroes. Her character of Sarah Connor in *The Terminator* is not only the mother of the 'saviour,' but in her actions alongside Reese and her final vanquishing of the T-800, she is also the saviour of the present. She's not presented as an especially heroic character (unlike, say, Ripley in *Alien* and *Aliens* who always appeared to have the potential to rise to the challenge of the alien creatures). Sarah Connor is a typical LA working-class woman, as established in the early character based scenes, faced with an unimaginable responsibility and a seemingly insurmountable adversary ("It absolutely will not stop," warns Reese of the Terminator). It's her very 'ordinariness' which is celebrated in *The Terminator*. Unlike the sequel, in the first film Connor does not sport the kind of action hero 'hard' body she later develops to tackle the coming storm. She's an example of 'ordinary' female empowerment, a solution just awaiting the problem in the form of Kyle Reese and the Terminator.

More than 50 years prior to Cameron's breakthrough movie, the great logician Kurt Godel invented a hypothetical universe consistent with Einstein's Theory of Relativity which allowed 'time loops' in which events in the future cause events in the past then cause their own causes! In *The Terminator*, a son sends his father back in time to save and inseminate his mother, so combining the insights of the greatest Austrian-American mind (Godel) with the talents of the greatest Austrian-American body (Schwarzenegger)!

Harlan Ellison Versus James Cameron: Knocking James Cameron off his perch as 'King of the World' mark one was an unexpected lawsuit from

SF author Harlan Ellison. Acclaimed author of such short story collections as *Deathbird Stories* and *Shatterday*, Ellison was then writing a movie review column for *The Magazine Of Fantasy And Science Fiction*. He'd been hearing tales about *The Terminator*'s resemblance to some of his own work during production of the film but waited until he'd seen the completed movie before following up. "It was not my desire to find similarity," stated Ellison in a 1998 interview. "I was sitting there, thinking 'Please, don't let it be...,' but if you look at the opening three minutes of my *Soldier* episode [of *The Outer Limits*] and the first three minutes of *Terminator*, they are not only similar, but exact. By the time I left, I knew I had a case against somebody who'd plagiarised my work."

Ellison wrote about the matter in April 1985 edition of his magazine column: "It has become necessary to say something about *The Terminator*. Yes, folks, I'm more than painfully aware that *The Terminator* resembles my own *Outer Limits* script *Soldier* in ways so obvious and striking that you've been moved to call me, write letters, send me telegrams and pass the gardyloo along by word of mouth with my friends. You really must cease waking me in the wee hours to advise me I've been ripped off. As I write this, attorneys are talking."

And so they were. "I loved the movie, was just blown away by it," claimed Ellison. "I walked out of the theatre, went home and called my lawyer." The concepts behind *The Terminator* bore an uncanny resemblance to not one, but three, works by Harlan Ellison. Two were his episodes for *The Outer Limits* SF anthology TV show. *Soldier*, broadcast in September 1964, told of two enemy participants in a future war transported back in time to 1960s urban America where they continue their battle. Ellison's screenplay was based on his own short story *Soldier From Tomorrow* published in the October 1957 issue of *Fantastic Universe Science Fiction*. The second episode was *Demon With A Glass Hand*, broadcast in October 1964. It drew on Ellison's developing Kyben mythology which he was exploring in a series of short stories. This tale featured a lone man from the future seemingly holding the secret of humanity's salvation. As it turns out the character of Trent (Robert Culp) is not a man at all, but a robot in the form of a man. The third Ellison work which featured significant aspects later matched by *The Terminator* was the short story *I Have No Mouth And I Must Scream*.

Ellison approached Hemdale and Orion through his lawyers, who in turn took the accusation to James Cameron. Cameron angrily defended himself, claiming that robots and time travel were common themes in science fiction. The studio offered to back Cameron in defending a court case against Ellison, but if Cameron lost the case, the studio and Orion would in turn sue the writer-director himself for misrepresentation. "What it came down to was: I could risk getting completely wiped out," recalled Cameron in the book *Dreaming Aloud*, "or I could wave it off and let this guy [Ellison] get his credit."

Cameron took the wiser path and settled the claim with Ellison. *The Terminator* was re-issued with a credit acknowledging the works of Harlan Ellison and the author was reportedly paid around $400,000. In an interview with Marc Shapiro, author of a biography of James Cameron, Ellison is reported to have said: "If Cameron had called me and said, 'I know your story, but I've got a different idea, do you mind if I do a variation on it?' I would have said, 'Go ahead, man, knock yourself out and have a good time.' All I would have asked for was a 'Thank You, Harlan Ellison' on the credit line next to the guy who brought the doughnuts. It wouldn't have cost him a penny..."

Trivia: The Terminator is a Cyberdyne Systems Model 101, Series 800 (T-800). A previous series, the T-600, had rubber skin and could be spotted easily up close. The humans who the machines rounded up and sent to death camps were branded with an identification bar code on the forearm, similar to the ID numbers tattooed onto victims of the holocaust. William Wisher Jr., an old high school friend of Cameron's, received a credit reading 'additional dialogue.' He wrote several scenes, specifically those with Lt. Traxler and Detective Vukovich. He also played the police officer who the Terminator attacks and steals a car from. He went on to be a fully credited co-writer on *Terminator 2: Judgment Day*.

The Verdict: 4/5

Aliens (1986)

"An executive told me he didn't like *Aliens* because it was wall-to-wall horror and needed more character development."

– James Cameron

Crew: Director: James Cameron; Writers: James Cameron, David Giler (story), Walter Hill (story); Producers: Gordon Carroll (executive producer), David Giler (executive producer), Walter Hill (executive producer), Gale Ann Hurd (producer); Original music: James Horner; Non-original music: Jerry Goldsmith (from *Alien* (1979), uncredited), Aram Khachaturyan (from *Ballet Suite Gayaneh*, uncredited); Cinematography: Adrian Biddle; Film Editing: Ray Lovejoy; Production Design: Peter Lamont; Art Direction: Ken Court, Bert Davey, Fred Hole, Michael Lamont; Set Decoration: Crispian Sallis; Costume Design: Emma Porteus (as Emma Porteous)

Cast: Sigourney Weaver (Lt. Ellen Ripley), Michael Biehn (Corporal Dwayne Hicks), Paul Reiser (Carter J Burke), Lance Henriksen (Bishop), Carrie Henn (Rebecca 'Newt' Jorden), Bill Paxton (Private Hudson), William Hope (Lt. Gorman), Jenette Goldstein (Private Vasquez), Al Matthews (Sgt. Apone), Mark Rolston (Private Drake), Ricco Ross (Private Frost), Colette Hiller (Corporal Ferro), Daniel Kash (Private Spunkmeyer), Cynthia Scott (Corporal Dietrich), Tip Tipping (Private T Crowe)

Plot: Marines in space, as Ripley (after 57 years in suspended animation) and a team of soldiers journey to a colony planet to battle the alien menace...

Inspiration: James Cameron's first attempt at writing a script – mainly to secure himself a directing assignment – had drawn him to the attention of several Hollywood studios needing a writer for hire. He'd worked on *Rambo, First Blood: Part 2,* but had found his work dumbed down by the film's star Sylvester Stallone. Offered the chance to direct the project, just before *The Terminator* entered production, Cameron turned it down as his heart wasn't in the material. That wasn't the case with *Aliens*, the sequel he was scripting to Ridley Scott's *Alien* (1979). "At that point I didn't really need to do an *Alien* sequel," claimed Cameron, "but I liked what I had created and once I had that imagery in my head I couldn't get rid of it any other way but to go out and make the movie."

Working from the three-word outline given to him by *Alien* producers Walter Hill and David Giler – "Ripley and soldiers" – Cameron concocted a sequel screenplay retaining what he thought were the best elements of the original, wrapping the whole thing up in a 'grunts in space' action movie.

The resulting 42-page treatment for *Aliens* was greeted with dismay by executives at 20th Century-Fox. They described the script as wall-to-wall horror which needed more character development. The revised treatment expanded the character of Ripley, giving her more of a backstory and also developed the characters of the fairly anonymous military types who go head to head with multiple aliens. The finished script was delivered in July 1984. Cameron was quickly offered the director's chair on the project, too.

Development: With pre-production looming on the project in March 1985, 20th Century-Fox decided that they didn't want Cameron's personal and professional partner Gale Ann Hurd producing the film. Just as she had leveraged him into directing *The Terminator*, Cameron refused to tackle the project without Hurd. A threat by both to walk off the project saw Fox quickly back down. Cameron pushed his advantage and insisted that he'd only do the film if the star of the original, Sigourney Weaver, returned as Ellen Ripley. "I didn't really want to do the sequel," Weaver told *People* magazine. "I was pretty sceptical of what I thought was an attempt to cash in on the success of the original. Why should I do this movie?" After a meeting with Cameron and Hurd, a screening of *The Terminator* and an assurance that the pair wanted to make the sequel more of a character movie, Weaver committed to the project.

In the middle of all this, Cameron and Hurd decided to get married. The couple flew to the Hawaiian island of Maui in April 1985, married and enjoyed a honeymoon while 20th Century-Fox negotiated with a lead actress who knew she was the director's one and only choice. Weaver won a salary of $1 million, compared to $35,000 for the first film, and the sequel's budget increased from the proposed $12 million (Cameron wanted $15 million) to $18 million.

Production: Filming on *Aliens* was set for September 1985 at London's Pinewood Studios. Cameron filled the cast of space marines and other characters with faces familiar from his first two movies, including would-be Terminator Lance Henriksen, Michael Biehn (replacing first choice James Remar, who clashed with Cameron) and Bill Paxton, who'd had little more than a bit part in *The Terminator*. Actress Jenette Goldstein, who won the role of ballsy Private Vasquez, responded to an open casting call in London where she was living.

On the design and special effects side of the production, with the alien creature concept original designer, Swiss artist HR Gieger, unwilling to work on the sequel, Cameron reunited with Stan Winston. Cameron also turned to 'visual futurist' Syd Mead (*Blade Runner*) for the hardware and Ron Cobb (*Star Wars*) to create the planetscapes.

Despite the $18 million budget and 14-week shooting schedule Cameron had on *Aliens*, he structured his screenplay and filming schedule to use his Corman training to squeeze every last cent out of his budget. Although now able to afford better high-end technology to realise his vision, Cameron would rather use simple but convincing model shots and in-camera effects instead of relying on post-production trickery to bring his alien worlds to life.

One obstacle Cameron ran up against was the leading lady he'd fought for, Sigourney Weaver. Now a star as a result of the first movie, Weaver was used to getting her own way. As a director, James Cameron was not renowned for his people skills. In this instance, he knew when to back off. "Sigourney absolutely had input," he admitted to *Starlog* magazine. "She had ideas about certain lines of dialogue and certain things that she thought she could say. We went through the entire script and did a sort of dialogue polish."

Despite her commitment to the project. Weaver was late reporting to the *Aliens* shoot because her work on the movie *Half Moon Street*, also shooting in London, was behind schedule. Cameron was forced to rejig his shooting plans, abandoning his intention to shoot the opening sequence in which Ripley is revived first, instead replacing it with a scene where the marines explore a processing station that has become the aliens' nest. Shooting on location at a disused Acton electricity station was delayed while dangerous asbestos had to be removed from the site. Things were not off to a great start on *Aliens*.

With a release date of July 1986 to meet, the filming process on *Aliens* was often hurried and fraught, with Cameron riding roughshod over actors, crew and his own producer (and now wife) Gale Ann Hurd. She had her own problems to deal with, including a British film crew not used to working with a female producer and the outlandish demands from an out-of-control director (who also happened to be her husband). Jenette Goldstein recalled many of the Hurd-Cameron clashes over the film: "They weren't dancing around each other because they happened to be married. They were able to separate the personal from the professional."

Shepherding his actors through physically demanding scenes (just carrying the outsize heavy guns was exhausting), ensuring that his designers and special effects crews were able to come up with creatures and environments which surpassed those of the first movie, and hoping that a coherent and action-packed film would emerge at the end of the process, served to keep James Cameron on his toes.

As production neared its end during the autumn of 1985, the LA-based special effects firm LA Effects Group failed to deliver a motion-control camera rig for shooting some of the action scenes. Cameron quickly turned to a local London outfit, Arkadon Motion Control, to step into the breach. The climax of the movie, the battle between Ripley and the 14-foot-tall Alien Queen, was the most fraught section of the shooting process and it was for this sequence that Cameron required the motion-control camera. What LA Effects Group claimed would take an additional four months to achieve, Cameron with Brian Johnson of Arkadon, who'd worked on *Alien* and *The Empire Strikes Back*, achieved in six weeks, completing the film a mere four weeks prior to its scheduled opening date.

The idea for the climatic power-loader sequence dated back to James Cameron's earliest film-making days, even before his work with Roger Corman. "When I was young and my friends and I did this little film with the $20,000 from the rich, Mormon dentists out in Orange County [*Xenon Genesis*], we came up with a number of visual set pieces," Cameron told *Omni* magazine. "The story we wanted took place on a colony starship bound for another planet with the last remnants of humanity frozen on board. I came up with a device I called 'the Spider' that was used to crawl around the outside of the ship to make repairs. It was a four-legged walking machine that used a tele-presence-type amplification: you put your feet in things, you grabbed onto these controls, and however you moved and walked, it duplicated your actions. It worked really well. It was an amazing piece of work for a bunch of dumbshits that didn't know what they were doing. A year and a half later, *The Empire Strikes Back* came out with these big walking machines in it. I felt vaguely ripped off, or scooped would be more accurate. So I changed 'the Spider' to more of an upright, forklift exoskeleton concept."

It was this new version of 'the spider' that Cameron would use in the climax of *Aliens*, a logical mechanical, technological device which would allow Ripley to get the better of the Alien Queen. Cameron at one stage thought of kitting out his Marines in mechanical battle suits (rather like the heroes of Robert Heinlein's *Starship Troopers*), but couldn't see a story reason for Ripley to know how to use one. "How would Ripley know how to operate a battle suit?" Cameron claims he asked himself. "[The Marines] wouldn't be teaching her. It was really critical to the story that she emerge under pressure as the person who really takes control. They discredit her at the beginning; the last thing they'd do is hand her a gun and teach her how to use a battle suit. If in the interim between the end of the previous film and the beginning of the action on board the ship in *Aliens*, she had had to support herself as a dockworker at Gateway Station it was logical to assume that she might know how to handle a basic piece of cargo-handling equipment. You had to set it up. You had to see her volunteer to help unload the ship and impress them all that she could do it. Otherwise you'd never believe that she could duke it out with the Alien Queen."

This scene was crucial to how the entire film would work, especially the line "Get away from her, you bitch" which Ripley delivers to get the Queen to relinquish Newt, the girl Ripley has been protecting throughout the film. "There are always certain things on every film that you're nervous about," noted Cameron to *Omni*. "You like the challenge. The challenge is, can I make the audience believe this? Then you're nervous about it the whole time, which is good. The more nervous you are, the more you're going to set it up and make it work. When the film opened, I went to the Egyptian Theatre in Hollywood. When the spaceship door came up, and there was Sigourney in the power loader, the audience went ape shit! That's what it's all about. It really taught me to not be afraid of the challenges, to find them, to seek them out because that's where the magic is."

Editing and post-production took place at Pinewood Studios immediately following the May 1986 wrap date for principal photography. Complex special effects shot were arriving at the editing room 'wet,' meaning barely completed in time. Composer James Horner was happy to have been asked to score the film but was horrified to discover that he had only 10 days to write 105 minutes of music. The movie was delivered to 20th Century-Fox in June 1986, with a running time of around two and a half hours. The studio insisted on a film of no more than two hours in duration and forced Cameron to cut back the movie, ditching almost 30 minutes of material (since restored in the *Aliens* Special Edition). The film was released with a running time of two hours and 17 minutes when Cameron insisted that to edit out any more would make the picture incoherent. The film opened as scheduled in July 1986.

Reception: 'Audiences will be riveted to their seats with drooling dread in anticipation of the next horrifying attack. The film is a worthy follow-up to Ridley Scott's 1979 shocker. Although the film accomplishes everything it aims to do, the overall impression is of a film made by an expert craftsman, while Scott clearly has something of the artist in him. Sigourney Weaver does a smashing job as Ripley, one of the great female screen roles of recent years. The strength with which she invests the part is invigorating, and the actress really gets down-and-dirty with tremendous flair.' – *Variety*. 'I am advising you not to eat before you see it.' – Roger Ebert, *Chicago-Sun Times*. '*Aliens* is a perfectly honourable sequel, taut and inexorably paced. It's blaster action rather than Gothic future horror.' – *The Los Angeles Times*. '*Aliens* met all the challenges that face a sequel and was ultimately able to stand on its own.' – *The Hollywood Reporter*. 'A touch less innovative than its predecessor.' – *The New York Times*

Box Office: From a budget of $18 million, *Aliens* went on to gross in excess of $85 million in its first US run, with a further $72 million abroad. It then grossed over $157 million worldwide.

Awards: Oscars won: Two (visual effects, sound effects editing); Oscar nominations: Seven (actress, editing, production design, score, sound, sound effects editing, visual effects).

Rep Company: Bill Paxton features as one of the main Marines, alongside *The Terminator*'s Michael Biehn. After being passed over for the mechanical man part of the Terminator, Henriksen was rewarded with a much more challenging android role in *Aliens*.

Analysis: It's toys for the boys (and girls) in *Aliens*, as Cameron takes Ridley Scott's understated original and ramps up the hardware factor. From ships and guns to flame-throwers and power loaders, the technology here is on the side of the humans and against the organic aliens, an exact reversal of the scenario in *The Terminator*.

In *Alien*, Ripley is a functioning member of the *Nostromo* crew, a crew where gender seems of little relevance. In Cameron's *Aliens*, however, Ripley is coded much more as an outsider. She comes from a different time, having spent 57 years in hibernation and been unable to warn that colonising the planet where the alien was discovered may not have been a great idea. Further, Ripley is a civilian on a military mission, not one of the core group of Marines. She has to repeatedly prove herself and win the respect of her colleagues in a way she didn't aboard the *Nostromo*. In the opening scenes, Vasquez dubs Ripley "Snow White," making explicit her status as feminised (unlike Vasquez, of whom Hicks asks "Have you ever been mistaken for a man?" Her reply: "No, have you?") and out of time (Snow White is put to sleep by the witch, just as Ripley was). However, unlike Snow White, Ripley doesn't wait to be rescued: she does the rescuing, saving the marines.

Additionally, burdening the character of Ripley with responsibility for Newt (she 'becomes' a mother, another feminising factor) makes possible the climatic face-off with the 'monstrous mother' of the Alien Queen. Both Ripley and the Queen are 'sole survivors' protecting their species (their offspring) from the other. The colonists have been wiped out by the aliens and the alien eggs are vaporised by Ripley. Just as Ripley kills the alien offspring (in the form of the eggs), so the Queen responds not by attacking Ripley but going after Newt (Ripley's figurative 'offspring'). The oppositions between the pair of mothers ("Get away from her, you bitch!") is complete. In the end, just as in *Alien*, it comes down to a simple battle for survival between Ripley and the Queen. However, in his expansion of the alien life cycle from the little shown in the original movie, James Cameron has emphasised the power of the feminine, in the same way he did with Sarah Connor in *The Terminator*. Each of the sequels (*Alien³* and *Alien Resurrection*) would build in different ways from these developments.

Trivia: Three different versions of the film have been released on video over the years: standard theatrical version (130 minutes), extended version (145 minutes, a shorter version of the Special Edition including the scenes that were cut from the standard version) and the Special Edition/Director's Cut (154 minutes). In the Special Edition, we get to see Ripley's daughter, Amanda McClarent Ripley, on a colour printout. The woman portrayed in this picture is in fact Sigourney Weaver's own mother, Elizabeth Inglis. The mechanism used to make the facehuggers thrash about in the stasis tubes in the science lab came from one of the flying piranhas in *Piranha II: The Spawning*. It took nine people to make the facehugger work, one person for each leg and someone for the tail. Cameron returned to Joseph Conrad (the inspiration for the ship name *Nostromo* in *Alien*) when it came to naming the ship Sulaco in *Aliens*. Sulaco was the town in which most of Joseph Conrad's book *Nostromo* took place.

The Verdict: 4/5

4. Back To The Future

The Abyss (1989)

"Everyone was running around screaming and pulling their hair out about how it was the most expensive movie in history, which of course it was not!"

– James Cameron

Crew: Director/Writer: James Cameron; Producers: Gale Ann Hurd (producer), Van Ling (producer, special edition); Original Music: Robert Garrett (additional music, special edition), Alan Silvestri; Cinematography: Mikael Salomon; Film Editing: Conrad Buff IV, Joel Goodman, Steven Quale (special edition), Howard E Smith; Casting: Howard Feuer; Production Design: Leslie Dilley; Art Direction: Russell Christian, Joseph C Nemec III; Set Decoration: Anne Kuljian; Costume Design: Deborah Everton

Cast: Ed Harris (Virgil 'Bud' Brigman), Mary Elizabeth Mastrantonio (Lindsey Brigman), Michael Biehn (Lieutenant Hiram Coffey), Leo Burmester (Catfish De Vries), Todd Graff (Alan 'Hippy' Carnes), John Bedford Lloyd (Jammer Willis), JC Quinn ('Sonny' Dawson), William Wisher Jr. (Bill Tyler)

Plot: Voyage To The Bottom Of The Sea meets *Close Encounters Of The Third Kind* as a group of oilmen and military types investigate a sunken sub only to encounter ET.

Inspiration: After the success of *Aliens*, Fox were keen to secure the further services of James Cameron in the hopes of producing another money-making blockbuster. For their part, Cameron and Hurd were just as keen to get back into production as soon as possible to cement their new-found position in Hollywood. It's an industry town where you're only as hot as your last movie.

Drawing inspiration from a story he'd written in High School, Cameron interested Hurd in putting together a movie about undersea exploration. Whilst President of the Science Club at school, Cameron had attended a presentation by commercial diver Frank Falejczyk, who had developed a way of breathing liquid oxygen. Inspired by that idea Cameron had drafted a tale of a group of divers based in an undersea science lab perched on an abyssal shelf. "It was really about scientific curiosity," Cameron claimed of his admittedly slight tale. "One by one, the crew descend the precipice using fluid breathing suits, and all are lost. At the end there's only one guy left, the lab's all wrecked and he goes out to see what happened to the others, knowing he's not going to come back. The story ends with him being drawn deeper and deeper by his curiosity," Cameron told author Paula Parisi in *Titanic And The Making Of James Cameron*. "I think I described it, in this bullshit high school way, as being like *The Tell-Tale Heart*, [with] a pulse at the bottom of the ocean..."

It would be 18 years on from 1970 before James Cameron would uncover this story to use as the basis of his next movie. "I waste nothing," Cameron told author Christopher Heard in *Dreaming Aloud*. "I can say quite honestly, though, that I tinkered with the story of *The Abyss* from the day that I wrote it when I was 17 until the day the special edition was released."

Based on the short story alone, Cameron and Hurd knew that actually making *The Abyss* was going to be a daunting prospect, but even they weren't prepared for what would soon be tagged the most difficult movie shoot in history. "*The Abyss* was really an all-or-nothing proposition," Gale Ann Hurd told Heard. "We either had to go with it right down the line or watch it collapse around us. We knew it was going to be tough going in, we just had no idea how tough..."

Development: Concerned that Fox had expressed worries about the $18 million budget for *Aliens* and that the proposed budget for *The Abyss*, based on an initial draft script, was around $50 million, James Cameron arranged to pitch the movie in person to studio bosses. Cameron and Hurd admitted their surprise that, in response to the lively pitch (and with the $157 million worldwide gross of *Aliens* fresh in their minds), Fox immediately greenlit pre-production on *The Abyss*.

In between *Aliens* and *The Abyss*, and determined to forge a production career for herself away from Cameron, Gale Ann Hurd had taken up the producer's role on *Alien Nation* (1988), a troubled SF thriller. When, in the Autumn of 1986, Cameron went to work on revising and developing the script for *The Abyss*, Hurd was elsewhere struggling to keep *Alien Nation* on track. The separation and the lull in their lives after *Aliens* had shown up cracks in their relationship. The pair were drifting apart emotionally, a state of affairs exaggerated by their professional separation.

As he approached writing the final draft of *The Abyss*, James Cameron was facing divorce for the second time. It was a theme he found himself irresistibly working into his storyline. "We were separated pending divorce when I asked her to produce *The Abyss*," Cameron told *US* magazine. As the script developed, the relationship between the characters of oilman Bud Brigman and his ex-wife Lindsey, whom he finds himself working with on a vast underwater undertaking, began to reflect his real-life situation.

When the script was finished, Cameron's attention was taken by another real-world underwater discovery. "When I was working on *The Abyss* the Titanic had just been discovered on the ocean floor. I met with Robert Ballard, the leader of the discovery team and I became infected with interest. I started reading about the [1912] event and the people and the story just started to appear quite naturally to me..."

There was another screenplay which distracted Cameron during this period. Gale Ann Hurd had run into trouble with the script for *Alien Nation*. Written by *Farscape* creator Rockne S O'Bannon, the tale of aliens integrating into society on Earth had undergone so many rewrites that the focus had been totally lost. As a result, Hurd turned to Cameron who dropped his work on *The Abyss* (with some relief) and his thoughts about the Titanic to do a complete rewrite on *Alien Nation*. "I don't think his heart was in it," O'Bannon told UK film and TV magazine *Dreamwatch*. "I know Gale and he were having problems. Some of the heart was taken out of [the story] and some of the more interesting and fun aspects of the film were homogenised. It just wasn't the usual magical James Cameron kind of thing..." Director Graham Baker agreed. "With Jim's script I felt we had lost the freshness and the ingenuity of the ideas and I was very disappointed with that." While the film ultimately failed at the box office, O'Bannon was able to explore some of the 'fun' of the concept and recapture the 'freshness and ingenuity' in a brief, but innovative, television series based on the movie.

After a further distraction directing a music video for obscure group Martini Ranch, Cameron returned to and completed the screenplay for *The Abyss*. Fox were happy with what they read and gave the go-ahead for a 140-day shoot and a budget of $50 million, even though some within the studio feared that sum would not be enough to realise the vision Cameron had committed to the page. Privately, Cameron himself had doubts about the task he'd set himself. "I just assumed I could infect everyone around me with my enthusiasm. People were going out of their way to tell me how crazy I was, but I kept telling them, 'Sure, it looks impossible on the surface, but we still have to do it.'"

Production: With a script in place and a four-month shooting schedule, the first major problem on *The Abyss* faced by Cameron and Hurd was where to shoot the demanding underwater and oil rig sequences. No existing studio facility would be able to cope with the variety of demands which Cameron's story would make and the prospect of shooting the film at various existing facilities (in Malta and the Bahamas) didn't appeal to Cameron or the studio who feared massive budget overruns as a result. "I toyed with the idea of constructing an underwater sound stage," admitted Cameron. "Then the specs and the costs came in and they were ridiculously high. Plan B had to be devised and it had to be devised quickly..."

Shooting in the open sea was sensibly ruled out. Cameron was an ambitious director who would drive himself and those around him in the production of *The Abyss*, but he was not altogether mad. "Too many problems," said Cameron of shooting at sea in an interview in *Omni*. "Possible hurricanes, sharks and teaching fish to act..."

The solution came from much closer to home than Malta or the Bahamas. Independent film-maker Earl Owensby had recently purchased an unfinished nuclear power plant built by the Duke Power Company in the 1970s in Gaffney, South Carolina, but lacked the funds to turn it into a functioning studio facility. A trip with Hurd and a survey team quickly revealed that the plant had big and deep enough spaces to be used for set building and shooting underwater. The containment vessel of the nuclear plant and the smaller turbine pit were converted into underwater sound stages, holding 7.5 million and 2.6 million gallons of water respectively. The bigger A-stage would house the Deepcore deep-sea oil drilling rig, the biggest submerged set ever built. With the addition of a water filtration system, sets were constructed in the plant's giant spaces then flooded with 10 million gallons of water. Cameron had his underwater studio.

Casting proved to be Cameron's next challenge. Where could he find actors willing to spend a large amount of shooting time wet and in water? Where would he find people willing to take part in a venture which included no small amount of risk to the participants? "The studio suggested that I cast a very big name in the lead role," Cameron told Christopher Heard. "They were adamant, until I said that casting the actor they were suggesting would add between six and eight million to the budget."

Cameron quickly turned to Michael Biehn, who'd featured in both *The Terminator* and *Aliens* as the first of his cast members on *The Abyss*. At least Biehn had an idea what a Cameron shoot would be like, even if this one was to prove to be the most extreme of them all. "Working with Jim Cameron provides an actor with an adventure, although I had to admit I really couldn't have imagined just how much of an adventure this one would end up being."

Having switched his leading characters from the scientists of his short story to the blue collar oil works and Navy SEALs of his screenplay, Cameron wanted actors who could capture those roles. Ed Harris, cast as Bud Brigman, was quickly taken by the project when he read the script. "I immediately got what Jim was trying to do: an action/adventure film that had a soul." However, Harris thought that stunt divers would be called upon to cover the more difficult aspects of the underwater filming. "I had no idea going in that I would be doing the kind of things in the movie that I ended up doing." Mary Elizabeth Mastrantonio was signed up for the female lead as Brigman's ex-wife Lindsey. "I was interested in the adventure this [film] was promising," she claimed. "I remember being hugely impressed by James Cameron when I met him. Before it was over, I'd wanted to kill him at least a dozen times..."

The filming facility wasn't the only technological development required by *The Abyss*. An underwater videotape system had to be developed so that Cameron could effectively direct the underwater action, and special helmets were designed for the actors which revealed their full faces and featured built-in lighting systems for more effective filming. They also allowed communication between the director and his actors (but not the other way around, Cameron evidently didn't like his cast to talk back to him, just follow his instructions). The helmets also allowed for recording of underwater dialogue. Cameron's approach to the problems of capturing his actors in genuine underwater environments was straightforward: "You will into existence something that wasn't there before. Propose problems that there aren't existing solutions to, and the smart people will say that just because a solution doesn't exist doesn't mean we can't make it exist..."

Production on *The Abyss* was behind from the first day of shooting because the Deepcore sets were not finished by the scheduled start date of 8 August 1988, so production was delayed until 20 August. When shooting did begin, the first day saw the newly-constructed underwater tank spring a leak. "It was just one thing after another," said Cameron in the book *Dreaming Aloud*. "The enormity of the undertaking never discouraged me. If anything, it encouraged me!"

All the main cast members and production crew on *The Abyss* had undergone a crash course diving programme in Los Angeles. After four weeks of diving instruction, even those who'd never set foot in the water before were certified to operate in deep-diving gear at depths of between 30 and 60 feet. However, the requirements of long days spent in and under the water, with the need to act and deliver dialogue as well, quickly began to take their toll on the cast. Ed Harris was one of the first to complain that he wasn't so much acting in *The Abyss* as surviving it. "It was pretty hairy," he told *The New York Times* in 1989. "The daily mental and physical strain was enormous." Mary Elizabeth Mastrantonio also complained of Cameron's focus on the technological toys featured in the movie. "If there was a toy and a human being in the same scene, the toy would get the close-up."

Long hours were spent preparing to film, then even longer hours were spent in the water tanks in an attempt to capture the shots needed. In developing new cameras and lighting systems (Cameron and his engineer brother Mike would gain five underwater camera patents from their work on *The Abyss*), Cameron was in his element, often overlooking the needs of his actors. Even Cameron loyalist Michael Biehn could see that the director was not focusing in the right place. "Jim was so impassioned about what he was doing that he was almost in a trance. I think he was often insensitive to actors of Ed and Mary's class. I don't think he realised how frustrating it is to get into make-up and costume and then spend the whole day waiting around..."

Cameron, though, escaped a mutiny by cast and crew by putting himself right where they were: in the depths. He'd undergone the same diving training course and was in the water as often as the actors and other production personnel, making a hands-on contribution to the filming of his epic. With filming sessions lasting anywhere between seven and 11 hours, Cameron and his cast would face a lengthy decompression period to avoid 'the bends.' Loathe to waste even one minute of time, Cameron would often be found hanging upside down, underwater, decompressing yet watching dailies (developed footage) from the previous shooting day through a glass panel in the tank.

Filming was to become more difficult as time progressed. To capture the dark depths of the deep sea, the water surface was covered by tarps and black beads. A freak hurricane destroyed the 200ft lid which was being used to black out A-tank. "Well, I guess we're on nights," was Cameron's only response, switching the shooting schedule to 7pm through to 7am each day.

Halfway through production one of the major pipes feeding the constantly recycling water through to A-tank burst. An investigation revealed that in a seeming effort to save money the contractor who'd converted the nuclear power plant containment chamber to a studio facility had used cheap plastic pipes which didn't accommodate pressured valves.

Stories of doom and disaster, of mistreatment of actors and unreasonable demands from the director, of crazy hours being worked in ridiculous situations, began to filter back to the Fox studio bosses in Los Angeles. The budget on the film had climbed from an initially agreed $37 million to $41 million and was now heading towards Cameron's initial estimate of $50 million – and the film wasn't even halfway through production with expensive post-production and special effects yet to come...

Fox felt it necessary to send a studio representative to the shooting of *The Abyss* in South Carolina to establish for themselves exactly what progress had been made on the film. Harold Schneider arrived in Gaffney, driving to the location in a limousine and with an entourage, according to Charlie Arneson, who was part of the underwater photographic team on *The Abyss*. Cameron made himself unavailable to meet with Schneider, leaving the studio executive to wander the facility in a none-too-subtle attempt to solicit stories of overruns and delays on the film. Six hours later, with shooting complete for the day, Cameron emerged from the underwater tank and went straight off to watch dailies rather than take time to talk with Schneider. Later, Cameron walked in on Schneider as he was interrogating more members of the production crew. As soon as the pair began talking, according to Arneson, the profanities began flying and it wasn't long until Cameron was physically threatening to tip Schneider over the edge of the diving platform into the water tank below. Schneider and his entourage made a quick retreat from the facility and returned to Hollywood. Cameron just turned to Arneson and said: "Sometimes you just have to make a point."

Cameron was to pay for his outburst. When signing on the dotted line to direct *The Abyss*, he'd committed to taking a cut in his own salary to cover any budget overruns, especially on special effects. Halfway through production, that clause was now invoked. "I'm not crazy about working for half price," journalist Marc Shapiro reported Cameron as claiming. However, he seems to have been realistic about where the responsibility for the situation on the film lay: "I can't absolve myself one hundred per cent. The director is responsible for the scope of the project."

Schneider's visit wasn't the last from a Fox executive. On a particularly trying day, when Cameron had nearly died after running out of air while diving (the second time Cameron had experienced a near-fatal incident on this film), Fox's newly-installed vice president of production Roger Birnbaum turned up. "I'd almost croaked," Cameron recalled in the Parisi *Titanic* book. "So Roger shows up, and he's going to solve all our problems. All I saw was a guy with a big bullseye on him." Before Birnbaum could resist, Cameron was fitting one of the deep-diving helmets on the surprised studio executive. "There was no air supply to the helmet, so he immediately starts thrashing around. I let him choke for about 20, 25 seconds, then I pulled the helmet off. 'That's what it feels like when you're running out of air... which happened to me a few hours ago. Shut the fuck up and go home.'"

It is from incidents like this whilst making *The Abyss* that the James Cameron legend has been built. "I've since learned to be more polite with my studio superiors," claims Cameron. During the course of filming *The Abyss*, Cameron lost the services of two assistant directors and was constantly under threat of his cast departing the project at a moment's notice. Most of the actors, including Michael Biehn and Ed Harris, suffered moments when they thought their lives were in danger. Biehn found himself weighted at the bottom of the tank with 10-15 minutes of oxygen left when there was a power cut. "Who knew how long we'd be down there," he recalled. "I suddenly realised I might not get out of there alive." During the scene in which Harris and fellow actor Leo Burmester were swimming, without air and suits, from one pod to another, Harris lost sight of the safety divers and suffered a moment's panic as he ran short of breath. Only the quick action of a vigilant safety diver saved the actor. Mary Elizabeth Mastrantonio, although never in physical danger herself, had her fair share of run-ins with the director, especially when he called for retake after retake of her trying resurrection scene.

Cameron was unrepentant about his treatment of the actors on *The Abyss*, whom he largely regarded as pawns needed for him to realise his vision. "I shed not a single tear for the actors," he told *The Los Angeles Times* in response to stories of what a monster he'd become on set. "Poor babies. It's the crew that's really busting their asses on this film. For the actors, most days the toughest thing they've had to do was to decide which magazine to read!"

As the troubled principal photography on *The Abyss* drew to a close, it seemed as though everyone on the shoot, from the director down to the catering, was on edge, just hoping that the nightmare would end. The film finally wrapped, two months behind schedule and several million dollars over the $50 million which James Cameron had expected to spend. Postproduction loomed, but before he could finish his movie, Cameron had to officially finish his marriage to Hurd. They'd become ever more distant, although never less than professional, as the production had dragged on. "There was nothing uncivil about the relationship between Gale and Jim," reported Mastrantonio, something that could not be said of her own relationship with her director. The long-anticipated divorce was finalised in February 1989. "I can't really say what it was that drove the wedge between Gale and me," ruminated Cameron. "But once it was there, it was there."

Post-production on *The Abyss* would be only slightly less fraught than the actual shooting. While the aliens discovered at the bottom of the sea had been realised through practical puppetry effects by Steve Johnson during shooting, they were augmented in post-production by computer-generated effects courtesy of Lucasfilm's special effects house Industrial Light & Magic (ILM), best know for the *Star Wars* movies. ILM and Cameron developed the water tentacle effect which was to pave the way for the later significant effects developments that would feature in Cameron's *Terminator 2*.

The biggest problem Cameron now faced, though, was the film's long running time. On *The Abyss* Cameron enjoyed contractual 'final cut,' something he'd claimed he'd always had in practice, except on *Piranha II*. Cameron sees having final cut as "a complicated thing, earned commercially and retained by responsible behaviour. I also think you get it through a kind of force of personality." Cameron's initial cut of *The Abyss* clocked in at 140 minutes, a good 20 minutes longer than the average summer blockbuster. The extra length came from a "philosophical, but spectacular" ending he'd shot for his film. One ending saw the aliens saving the principal characters, while the other saw them threatening mankind with giant tidal waves as a way of warning them about from killing each other and the planet. "By having the ending I wanted, I would be delivering a movie that would be much longer than I was contractually obligated to deliver. The studio wanted the movie to be two hours long and no more," stated Cameron in *Dreaming Aloud.* As the June 1989 release date loomed, the film was test-screened with the 'tidal wave' ending, earning a mixed response from the audience in Dallas, Texas. Cameron recut the film to incorporate elements of both endings, resulting in a two hour and 20 minute film. The release was moved to late July and the new cut was tested again before a sneak preview audience. It was a process which Cameron didn't enjoy or approve of, but as he was in a genuine quandary about how to reconcile the two endings he'd shot, he went with it. The 'tidal wave' sequence was removed. "I had shot some very large, very expensive scenes for an ending that I wanted for the movie," noted Cameron. These scenes were reinstated in the 1996 Special Edition of the film. The truncated version of *The Abyss*, lacking the tidal waves, was finally released on 9 August 1989, in the wake of two more underwater monster movies, *Deepstar Six* and *Leviathan*, both of which had sunk without trace at the box office. The film had an uphill struggle to attract an audience. "I wouldn't say it failed," claimed Cameron, "but we came out the same weekend as *Uncle Buck* and made less money," – $54 million for *The Abyss* compared to $64 million for *Uncle Buck* – "but who remembers *Uncle Buck* today? People are still watching *The Abyss*."

Despite the problems involved, James Cameron was content that he'd done the best job in making *The Abyss* that he possibly could. "What it comes down to is that I simply couldn't not do it," he said of the film. "I had to see this movie and the only way to see it was to go out and make it. Would I go through that whole experience again, knowing what I know now? Absolutely." Ed Harris, for one, might disagree...

Reception: 'A first-rate underwater suspenser with an other-worldly twist, *The Abyss* suffers from a pay-off unworthy of its build-up. James Cameron delivers riveting, supercharged action segments only to get soggy when the aliens turn out to be friendly. When the pic arrives at its major metaphorical question – what lies at the bottom of the abyss? – it flounders. Cameron hasn't got the answers, only a vague, optimistic suggestion.' – *Variety*. 'The best way to enjoy this overwrought action film is to go in knowing that it is spectacularly silly... Cameron offsets his pretentious themes with luminous underwater photography, extraordinary special effects and countless near-catastrophes.' – *The New York Times*. '*The Abyss* is the most hardware-cluttered movie imaginable, yet it leaves you feeling sappily euphoric. It's not hard to imagine that James Cameron has carried this film in his head since he was 17. It's a 17-year-old's vision.' – *The Los Angeles Times*. 'In *The Abyss*, Cameron seems utterly lost. He is trying to reach further down into himself and everything he clutches at runs through his fingers.' – *The New Yorker*. 'The only summer movie that doesn't dilute its tension with irony. It's thrilling, dumb and irresistible.' – *Newsweek*. '*The Abyss* reaches for the mood of an epic, but even on its tippy-toes its reach is not quite up to its grasp.' – *The Los Angeles Weekly*.

Box Office: Widely regarded as a critical and commercial failure, *The Abyss* opened to a weekend box-office take of $9.3 million, but sank rapidly, barely managing to recoup the original cost of $41 million spent making the film. It was only through video and DVD sales of both the original, but especially of the Special Edition that *The Abyss* was able to be considered a financial success by Fox. The Special Edition also went some way to rehabilitating the film in the eyes of the critics. Domestic US box office eventually reached $85 million, with an additional $46 million accrued overseas.

Awards: Oscars won: One (visual effects); Oscar nominations: Four (visual effects, art direction, cinematography, sound).

Rep Company: Michael Biehn is the only member of the regular Cameron crew to sign on for duty on *The Abyss*.

Analysis: Cameron's sense of wonder and people-meet-machines theme reached a personal pinnacle in *The Abyss*. From the *Boy's Own* adventure to the simplistic Cold War politics and take on global issues, *The Abyss* is an adventure for teenagers, seemingly made by a teenager pretending to be a grown-up film-maker (which may also explain some of Cameron's outlandish on-set behaviour). The Cold War politics are mirrored in the cold war relationship between Bud and Lindsey. Despite being based on Cameron's own real-life situation, in the form of a 1980s film, the emotions are as unreal as the underwater aliens.

Cameron films every submarine and underwater installation like the UFOs in Steven Spielberg's *Close Encounters Of The Third Kind*. Light and colour combine to capture the other-worldly nature of deep-sea exploration, with Cameron equating the unknown and unknowable bottom of the ocean with deep space. At first it might seem an odd approach to take, but with the surprising twist that aliens are lurking deep in the sea, it makes sense. The sheer number of machines and amount of high-tech equipment swamps the human characters in *The Abyss* to such an extent that the film sometimes seems to be more computer game than movie.

The fusion of a personal relationship story in the middle of what turns out to be a global threat doesn't work terribly well, but in this respect *The Abyss* seems like a dry run for *Titanic*. (In fact, *Titanic* would seem to be in large part a spiritual sequel to *The Abyss*.)

A prime example of 1980s overblown movie-making, *The Abyss* is perhaps best remembered for its production process rather than the final result. However, in forming the myth of James Cameron the overblown and out-of-control director, it paved the way for those 1990s 'sons of Cameron,' Michael Bay (*Pearl Harbour*) and Simon West (*Lara Croft: Tomb Raider*). Whether or not that's a good thing...

The Abyss Special Edition: After the huge success of *Terminator 2*, James Cameron was able to return to *The Abyss* and revise the only one of his major films to fail to be a box-office hit. Signing a development/production deal between his company Lightstorm and Fox allowed him to recut and re-release the longer version of *The Abyss*, dubbed the Special Edition, in 1992. "It was really a no-win situation," he recalled. "If we release a special edition and it flops, then we've bombed twice with the same movie. If we release it and it turns out to be a huge success, then we look like dopes for not putting it out in the first place..."

This wasn't just a case of reinstating the tidal wave sequence. Cameron recut the entire film, resulting in actors returning to redub dialogue, new music being added and extra special effects being worked in.

The tidal wave sequences, particularly, required more attention, to make the water appear suspended in the air but still free-flowing. "That was critical because if you thought it was just a big still frame, a freeze frame, it wouldn't have had any real power. The idea that it was still living water suspended was a much more powerful and surreal image. Truthfully, when we made the film in 1989 we couldn't quite get that," Cameron told *Omni*.

Even though it gave him a chance to finally realise his initial vision, James Cameron had reservations about releasing a different version of *The Abyss*. "I was very ambivalent about a Special Edition of *The Abyss*. A lot of people were curious about the wave scene, but I felt that we'd made a decision to go a certain way for the release. Why second-guess that? I said if we're going to do it, the only thing that would make it exciting for me is if we do it [release it as a] film. Let's make a couple of prints, stick them in theatres, and see if we can attract some critical attention to the film in its three-hour version. People have criticised this kind of 'alternate reality' versions of films as being an attempt to squeeze the last drop of blood out of a turnip. *The Abyss* project was pretty high-minded because we didn't go into it thinking that we were going to make any money. If we broke even, we'd be happy."

Trivia: The scene with the water tentacle was written so that it could be removed without interfering with the story because no one knew whether the effect would work successfully. The actors interacted with a length of heater hose held up by a member of the crew. During the TV news report of the US and Russian ships colliding, the accompanying pictures are of ships from the British Task Force hit during the Falkland Islands campaign. Cameron was forced to cut the pre-credits Nietzsche quote '...when you look long into an abyss, the abyss also looks into you,' from the original theatrical release because the movie *Criminal Law* (1988) had used it, and Cameron didn't want to seem like an imitator. The quote was restored in the director's cut.

The Verdict: 3/5

Terminator 2: Judgment Day (1991)

"I have everything to lose and nothing to gain on this film. If *Terminator 2* fails, I could be in big trouble."

– James Cameron

AKA *T2 (1991)*

Crew: Director: James Cameron; Writers: James Cameron, William Wisher Jr. (as William Wisher); Producer: Stephanie Austin (co-producer), James Cameron (producer), Gale Ann Hurd (executive producer), Mario Kassar (executive producer), BJ Rack (co-producer); Original music: Brad Fiedel; Cinematography: Adam Greenberg; Film Editing: Conrad Buff, Dody Dorn (special edition), Mark Goldblatt, Richard A Harris; Casting: Mali Finn; Production Design: Joseph C Nemec III; Art Direction: Joseph P Lucky; Set Decoration: John M Dwyer; Costume Design: Marlene Stewart

Cast: Arnold Schwarzenegger (The Terminator, T-800), Linda Hamilton (Sarah Connor), Edward Furlong (John Connor), Robert Patrick (T-1000), Earl Boen (Dr Peter Silberman), Joe Morton (Miles Bennett Dyson), Jenette Goldstein (Janelle Voight), Don Stanton (Lewis, the Guard), Dan Stanton (Lewis as T-1000), Michael Biehn (Kyle Reese, Special Edition); William Wisher Jr. (Galleria Photographer, uncredited)

Plot: A T-800 Terminator is on a new mission, this time to protect Sarah Connor and her teenage son John, from the attentions of the T-1000, a more sophisticated future assassin.

Inspiration: By July 1990 James Cameron was in a position to set up his own film production company, which he named Lightstorm after the lightning effects which greeted the arrival of Arnold Schwarzenegger in *The Terminator*. The aim was to give Cameron even more control over his own films, especially after his dealings with Fox on the final cut of *The Abyss*. Former video executive Larry Kasanoff was hired to run the company on Cameron's behalf.

Cameron wanted a sequel to *The Terminator* to be the first Lightstorm production. The success of the first film ensured that any sequel would be as close to a sure-fire hit as was possible in Hollywood. However, he was equally wary of being typecast as a director of big-budget SF and nothing else. In an attempt to avoid that fate, Cameron set about developing some non-SF projects, including a real-life multiple personality disorder drama called *The Crowded Room*. He also made an attempt to untangle the legal situation surrounding the movie rights for the Marvel superhero character

Spider-Man. Despite the investment of much time and effort, neither of these projects progressed very far or very fast, a situation Cameron was unused to...

Cameron was also interested in working with actress Jamie Lee Curtis, so he visited the filming of her new thriller *Blue Steel* (1990). While he'd later work with the actress on *True Lies*, it was the director of the film, Kathryn Bigelow, who caught Cameron's eye. He'd heard of her from Bill Paxton and Lance Henriksen who'd worked on the Bigelow-directed *Near Dark* (1987) and was immediately taken with her when they met. Their relationship developed very quickly and by the time she'd finished shooting *Blue Steel* the pair were married in August 1989. As his wife prepared *Riders On The Storm* (later titled *Point Break*), which Cameron would produce, he set about drafting a sequel to *The Terminator*.

Cameron had problems coming up with ideas for the follow-up to the unexpected hit. "I had told the story with the first film and there really wasn't a whole lot left to say," claimed Cameron of his initial approach to what would become *Terminator 2: Judgment Day*. "Arnold always seemed more enthusiastic about a sequel than I was," he told *Starlog* magazine in 1991.

The rights to *The Terminator* were held by Hemdale and Gale Ann Hurd, neither of whom were in a hurry to give them up or work again with James Cameron on his terms. Cameron had to play a waiting game until Hemdale, in financial trouble, proved willing to sell off the rights to Carolco, a then-newish big-budget producer backing Cameron's plans. Carolco was also able to buy Hurd's interest in *The Terminator* property too. All that remained was for Cameron to come up with a suitable story. For that he contacted William Wisher, his long-time friend who'd helped out in developing the original *Terminator* plot and who'd co-written *The Terminator* novelisation. "Jim had an idea, basically a couple of sentences: 'Young John Connor and the Terminator who comes back to befriend him,'" claimed Wisher in *Starlog*.

The pair were quickly able to work up a treatment for the sequel based around this amusing 'a boy and his Terminator' notion. By this time Arnold Schwarzenegger's career had developed and changed so much that it seemed unlikely he'd be willing to play the villain of the piece... Cameron had to find a way to turn his Terminator character into a hero, so had the idea of the Schwarzenegger model Terminator protecting John Connor while a new, more deadly breed of Terminator would be sent to kill him. The problem was, how could they come up with a foe who would be more formidable than Arnold Schwarzenegger? One idea would see Schwarzenegger play both Terminators, but that was felt more likely to lead to audience confusion. Instead of building a bigger and more fearsome creature which would tower over Schwarzenegger, Cameron decided to return to his original idea of the Terminator as an infiltration unit, an average looking man able to blend into any surroundings. Thus the T-1000 was born.

Development: With Schwarzenegger and Cameron on board and Carolco willing to back the movie to the tune of $90 million (even though Cameron had estimated his original script would cost nearer $200 million to realise), *Terminator 2* was soon in production.

Casting began with Cameron trying to convince Linda Hamilton to return to reprise the role of Sarah Connor. Although he had a plan in mind to make the movie without the character if she refused to return, Cameron felt that the character's reappearance was crucial. He wasn't willing to turn in the final draft of the script until Carolco had a deal finalised with Hamilton. For her part, having had a tough time on the first movie, Hamilton was reluctant to work with Cameron again. Like Sigourney Weaver on *Aliens*, she knew her participation was important to the success of the movie, so she held out for the best financial deal she could get before signing on the dotted line.

With Hamilton on board, Cameron and Wisher set about cutting their script to a more manageable budget and length (the first draft was timed at around three and a half hours). "In the draft we put in every possible scene we wanted to see, even though we knew some of them would be cut for time and money [reasons]," said Cameron. "Although we loved these scenes because they not only gave us a chance to show what was only referred to in the first film – namely the fall of Skynet and the time displacement equipment – we knew that this was all essentially backstory, and we wanted to get to the main story in the present day as soon as possible and hit the ground running." Cut from the script were a detailed sub-plot focusing on Miles Dyson, the inventor of Skynet, some of Sarah Connor's training scenes and a scene which would see the adult John Connor sending Kyle Reese back in time (to the story of the original *Terminator*), in the knowledge that the other man was destined to become his father and die in the past... Before finishing the *Terminator 2* screenplay, Kathryn Bigelow had Cameron do a rewrite on the *Point Break* screenplay too.

With a script in place, production on *Terminator 2* was announced in May 1990 at the Cannes Film Festival in France, with a set release date of 4 July 1991. Now all Cameron had to do was make the movie...

Production: Casting moved forward quickly when James Cameron returned to the USA. He secured the services of Joe Morton for the pivotal role of Miles Dyson and signed up Robert Patrick, a relatively unknown actor later to star on the TV series *The X-Files*, to play the metamorphing T-1000, the second Terminator in the film. The biggest problem was finding a 14-year-old to fill the role of the young John Connor, future leader of the resistance to the machines' domination of mankind.

James Cameron and *T2* casting director Mali Finn saw hundreds of likely teen actors, but Cameron felt that the pretty boys of Hollywood he was seeing one after the other were not right for the troubled teen character he had in mind. Only one really caught his attention: Edward Furlong, found at the Pasadena Boys Club. Furlong had no acting experience and was so nervous he'd already fumbled one audition with Linda Hamilton, but the boy's genuineness struck a chord with Cameron. "Every actor I saw after Eddie seemed fake by comparison," Cameron said. Cameron took something of a leap in casting Furlong, but it was an instinctive move which was to pay off handsomely.

Before shooting could begin, Linda Hamilton had to work with a physical trainer, as well as undergoing weapons training, to get into shape for what would prove to be a demanding role. Edward Furlong was sent to a dialogue and acting coach to prepare the inexperienced actor for life on a James Cameron film.

Primed by the reports which had emanated from the South Carolina shooting of *The Abyss*, the media in Los Angeles (both the film trade press and the mainstream press) were ready to chronicle the latest out-of-control project from megalomaniac director James Cameron. With a budget set at over $90 million by the first day of shooting (at a time when the average film budget was in the region of $30 million), the media would find rich pickings. Two of the main problems which frustrated Cameron during shooting and led to much of his yelling at actors came from his two stars: Furlong and Schwarzenegger. Cameron found himself paying the price for hiring the inexperienced Furlong. While the final result would make the struggle worthwhile, Cameron did find guiding the young non-actor a trying process. Additionally, Schwarzenegger discovered his previously stoic and near-silent Terminator had now become a more talkative character who was having to show emotions in the new twist on the character which Cameron and Wisher had developed. Repeated multiple takes of individual scenes quickly became the rule of thumb on *Terminator 2*.

The stories of Cameron's outlandish behaviour soon mounted up, including a threat to fire a crew member who took a toilet break, his habit of making the cast and crew work through lunch breaks and his rigging up of a loudspeaker system so everyone on the set or location could hear his instructions (or his verbal assaults on other members of the crew). T-shirts were quickly printed and worn by members of the crew bearing the slogans: 'You Can't Scare Me, I Work For James Cameron' and '*Terminator 3*: Not With Me!' Actor Joe Morton witnessed several of the director's trademark outbursts, but unlike on earlier films the actors got off lightly. "He was great with the actors," said Morton. "It was the crew that bore the brunt of his abuse."

Cameron had his own explanation for his characteristic approach to filmmaking. "I'm harsh on people because I want to inspire them to do their very best," he explained. "This is a business, not a party. Some people take it personally and some people don't. The ones who work with me again are the ones who don't."

Despite their marriage being relatively new, the professional commitments of James Cameron and Kathryn Bigelow were already taking their toll. Deep in production on *Terminator 2* Cameron tried to stay in touch with Bigelow who was equally deep in production on *Point Break*. Forced by their jobs to spend so much time apart, it was clear that the professional pressures which had dissolved the Cameron-Hurd partnership were very much still in evidence. It was no surprise, then, that stories of a relationship between Cameron and his leading lady on *Terminator 2*, Linda Hamilton, began to replace tales of budget-busting effects and action sequences, and directorial abuse, on the front pages of Los Angeles' newspapers.

Denials were immediately forthcoming from Cameron, but in a 1991 interview Hamilton hinted that this time around she'd found her director to be a different man. "This time I found him wonderful to work with," she told *The Los Angeles Village View*. "There was a lot of growth on his part. He certainly is learning to work with actors. I guess you could say that this time we bonded. I've come to appreciate him more..."

Planned like a military operation to ensure there was a finished film to meet the studio-imposed release date, shooting on *Terminator 2* began on 9 October 1990 in the Palmsdale desert. Entirely shot in California, the production found good use for some distinctive and some familiar locations. From the LA storm drains and the flood control channel of the San Fernando Valley (where the chase between the truck driven by the T-1000 and the bike ridden by Schwarzenegger and Furlong was shot) to the disused Lake View Terrace Medical Centre (the mental hospital in which Sarah Connor is incarcerated) and a crowded shopping mall in Santa Monica, the production team crossed California. It was not surprising that about 100 days into the shooting schedule Cameron and his 200-strong team were beginning to fray at the edges. Shooting scenes featuring Michael Biehn and Linda Hamilton at the end of a day when nothing had gone right, Cameron found himself sitting starring into space rather than barking out orders at his crew. Lack of sleep and the emotional and physical toll of the outsize monster that is a James Cameron film production had finally caught up with the director himself.

There was no time to stop and rest, however, because the clock was counting down to the release date of 4 July 1991. There was much still to be done. A dormant steel mill had been located in Fontana, California, to serve as the location for the film's climax. The only catch was that filming had to be completed before the entire mill was dismantled and shipped to China by its new owners. Another challenge was finding an office complex to double as the Cyberdyne HQ, which could be destroyed for the purposes of the film. An empty office complex in Fremont, California, was finally located. On the evening of the shooting of the major sequence featuring countless police cars, a helicopter, hundreds of extras and several major explosions, the employees of several neighbouring buildings held a barbecue party on the roof of the building opposite the action. A false third floor facade had been constructed on the building by the art department, who'd also completed a fully built lobby for a key scene. Special effects co-ordinator Tommy Fisher and his team rigged the second floor of the building with a series of 55-gallon gasoline drums backed with sandbags for the big blowout.

While the main shoot was progressing, four major visual effects houses and several smaller suppliers were hard at work developing the groundbreaking special effects for which *Terminator 2* would be rightly famous. Over 300 optical and mechanical effects shots were required for the film and the only way they could be completed in time for the release date was for them to be produced simultaneously with the main live action shoot. The opening 'future war' sequence – a more elaborate version of the action glimpsed in the original film – was again handled by Gene Warren's Fantasy II Film Effects. He was also responsible for the crashing-tanker shots at the climax, a miniature effect which went hideously wrong on the first take and had to be re-rigged at massive expense. Oscar-winners Robert and Dennis Skotak's 4-Ward Productions handled the realisation of Sarah Connor's nuclear blast nightmare, involving the destruction of large-scale miniatures of prominent LA buildings. They also did some work on the T-1000 effects in the steel mill sequences. The other two companies – ILM and Stan Winston Studios – faced the film's greatest challenge: bringing the T-1000 to cinematic life.

The character would be realised through a combination of Robert Patrick's performance (which he duplicated almost naked and covered in blue stick-on reference points for the computer-generated imagery), mechanical puppets and prosthetics, and computer-created and augmented visuals. This character was so important to the success or failure of the film that Cameron arranged the production schedule to give both companies the longest possible lead time on the project.

Not only was James Cameron directing the main live action unit, he was also supervising the work of the second unit team, keeping a check on the progress of the special effects work and beginning work on the editing of scenes for the final cut. It's no small wonder the man was tired and hadn't collapsed totally by the time that shooting finished on 4 April 1991. "The most important thing was to stay on top of it while we were shooting, editing scenes as they were being shot," said Cameron. "I had to realise that I simply wasn't going to get a day off until the movie was in theatres, that was a given. It was not only a logistically difficult picture, a technologically difficult picture and a dramatically difficult picture, but it also had to be done on a ridiculously short schedule. So, what else is new?" Cameron described the looming short post-production schedule on *T2* as "the next phase of Hell" to *The Los Angeles Times*.

Three separate editing teams worked on the almost one million feet of footage which Cameron had shot. The teams were headed up by Conrad Buff (who'd worked on *The Abyss*), Richard Harris and Mark Goldblatt (who'd cut the original *Terminator* movie). First to hit the cutting room floor was the Sarah Connor-Kyle Reese dream sequence, much to the consternation of Linda Hamilton. Hamilton felt she'd put her heart and soul into the scene, which had been difficult to shoot and had taken many hours of heavy emotional work. "I was told that these scenes were an interruption to the pace of the movie," lamented Hamilton. She was angry that she didn't discover Cameron's decision to dispense with the scene until late on in post-production: "I was sleeping with the man and he didn't tell me, until we were looping [re-recording dialogue]. There was so much work that had gone into that love scene with Michael Biehn. You were brought into the open heart of the character, which is just never that wide open throughout the rest of the movie."

Cameron and Hamilton's relationship had flourished as shooting on *T2* had drawn to a close. During the post-production phase he began moving his belongings from the West LA home he shared with Kathryn Bigelow into Hamilton's home. The relationship was an open secret in Hollywood and among the media, but Cameron publicly maintained that his marriage to Bigelow was fine.

Despite the relationship with Hamilton, another scene which had seen her suffering under old age make-up was dropped from the film. This final shot saw an older Sarah recalling how the rise of the machines had been averted and Judgment Day had not come. Cameron himself was very attached to the scene, but Carolco president Mario Kassar wanted it removed as it was both superfluous to the film and closed off the possibility of a further sequel. Cameron decided that the votes of an audience at a test screening would be used to decide if the scene stayed: he gambled that his choices would match those of his audience and lost (just as he had done on *The Abyss*). The scene went, but was later made available as an extra on the 'Ultimate' DVD release of *Terminator 2*.

The race was finally over and *Terminator 2: Judgment Day* made its release date of 4 July 1991 with a running time of 136 minutes.

Reception: 'A science fiction film with verve, imagination and even a lit-tle wit.' – *The Guardian*. '*Terminator 2* is half a terrific movie: the wrong half. For a breathless first hour, the film zips along in a textbook display of plot and showmanship. Then it stumbles over its own ambitions before set-tling for a conventional climax with a long fuse.' – *Time*. 'More elaborate than the original, but just as shrewdly put together. It cleverly continues its most successful elements.' – *The Los Angeles Times*. 'Cameron has made a swift, exciting special effects epic that justifies its vast expense and improves upon the first film's potent but rudimentary visual style.' – *The New York Times*. '*T2* is a jolt of 100 per cent pure adrenaline, a breathtaking work that redefines the boundaries of special effects and state-of-the-art action films.' – *The Los Angeles Village View*. 'More a remake than a sequel and less an homage than an obliteration.' – *Village Voice*. 'Among the most exciting spectacles ever.' – *New York Magazine*.

Box Office: Almost half the total number of movie tickets sold over the holiday weekend of 4 July 1991 were bought for *Terminator 2*, giving the film an opening weekend box-office take of $52.3 million. At the US domestic box office alone, the film would go on to gross in excess of $200 million, with an additional $284 million at the foreign box office, eclipsing the film's budget of just $90 million.

Awards: Oscars won: Four (sound, sound effects editing, visual effects, make-up); Oscar nominations: Six (sound, sound effects editing, visual effects, make-up, editing, cinematography).

Rep Company: Returning from the original *Terminator* were Linda Hamilton, Arnold Schwarzenegger and (in the special edition) Michael Biehn. Almost unnoticed, though, is a cameo by Jenette Goldstein (*Aliens'* private J Vasquez) as John Connor's adoptive mother.

Analysis: Technology never stands still. That's something that's clear from all of James Cameron's films, where a standing wave effect not possible in 1989 can be completed for *The Abyss* special edition in 1992. The same is true for the fictional world of *The Terminator*. The threat in the sequel is not a mere machine with moveable parts, but an inorganic metallic compound able to adopt almost any form. The special effects technology had advanced far enough (from the water tentacle experiments on *The Abyss*) by the time of *Terminator 2* to be able to show this concept, so it became central to the fiction of the follow-up narrative.

The sequel humanises the technological threat from the first movie: this Terminator learns and so becomes more human. This time, technology can be used against the T-1000 Terminator, but only once it has been adjusted to become more like us, more like its creators, in our own image. The T-1000 is a machine created by a machine and therefore has no need to maintain the 'human' image, other than practical necessity. The 'original' Terminator (T-800, Schwarzenegger) was created in mankind's own image, but lacked his empathy...

Throughout the sequel, it is young John Connor, the future resistance leader, who imparts his own naïve wisdom to the other main characters. It's John who reprograms the Terminator to learn to be human, to smile and instructs him not to kill. It is also John Connor who persuades his own mother to refrain from killing Miles Dyson, inventor of Skynet, the computer which launches the war which leads to the hegemony of the machines in the future.

The threat from the Terminator in the first film ("It absolutely will not stop," says Kyle Reese) becomes its virtue in the sequel. Considering the suitability of the Terminator as a protector for John, Sarah Connor sees this relentlessness (which previously threatened her) as a benefit. "The Terminator would never stop. It would always be there and it would protect him," muses Connor in voice-over. She concludes that the man-machine could be the "best father" for John. In a role reversal (one of many: the evil Terminator is disguised as a figure of authority, an LA policeman, while the good Terminator is a leather-clad biker) Sarah Connor becomes the dehumanised Terminator in her stalking and attempted assassination of Miles Dyson. It's only in renouncing her new 'hard' body and self-imposed lack of emotion, through her son's intervention, that Sarah Connor can become human again.

The ultimate humanisation of the Terminator is realised by its death, its capacity for self-sacrifice. Realising he contains the only remaining example of the computer chip which makes machine intelligence possible, the T-800 protector Terminator allows itself to be destroyed (against John Connor's wishes) rather than allow the possibility that the cycle be perpetuated. In *Terminator 2*, the triumph of the human is entirely dependent on the humanisation of the machine.

Trivia: The sounds of dog food oozing out of cans and microphones being slammed into buckets full of yoghurt were used to create the sound effects of the T-1000 changing shape and taking bullet hits. Actor Robert Patrick walks with a slight limp, from an old sports injury. Dennis Muren's team incorporated it into the computer-generated shots of the T-1000. The tow truck in the storm drain was driven part of the time by a hidden driver. Robert Patrick was on the right side with a fake steering wheel. The licence plate was mirrored, so that when the shot was reversed everything looked correct. They accidentally filmed a street sign. The computer effects team reversed the sign in post-production. In some other shots the cracked windshield hid the stunt driver's face. The Terminator tricks the T-1000 by asking why 'Wolfie' is barking. The dog's real name is Max, but James Cameron once had a dog named Wolfie. The pumps at the gas station the characters spend the night in have the logo for Benthic Petroleum, the company from *The Abyss*. The truck with the liquid nitrogen also sports this logo. Linda Hamilton's twin Leslie Hamilton Gearren played the T-1000 when it was imitating Sarah. Leslie is also in a mirror scene that is only in the Special Edition. Despite the opportunity with the Special Edition, there were some scenes which Cameron did not reinstate. After killing the dog the T-1000 searches John's room for clues. He moves his fingers along the wall, feeling for clues, and find some hidden photographs of John and Sarah. This scene is not in the Special Edition DVD of the movie, but is included as an additional extra. Cameron cut it because he thought it was redundant.

The Verdict: 4/5

5. Into The Deep

True Lies (1994)

Crew: Director: James Cameron; Writers: James Cameron (screenplay), Claude Zidi, Simon Michaël and Didier Kaminka (screenplay *La Totale!*); Producer: Stephanie Austin (producer), James Cameron (producer), Pamela Easley (associate producer), Lawrence Kasanoff (executive producer), Rae Sanchini (executive producer), Robert Shriver (executive producer); Original music: Brad Fiedel, Frederick Loewe (song *Camelot*); Cinematography: Russell Carpenter; Film Editing: Conrad Buff, James Cameron (uncredited), Mark Goldblatt, Richard A Harris; Casting: Mali Finn; Production Design: Peter Lamont; Art Direction: Robert W Laing, Michael Novotny; Set Decoration: Cindy Carr; Costume Design: Marlene Stewart

Cast: Arnold Schwarzenegger (Harry Tasker/Harry Renquist/Boris), Jamie Lee Curtis (Helen Tasker), Tom Arnold (Albert 'Gib' Gibson), Bill Paxton (Simon), Tia Carrere (Juno Skinner), Art Malik (Salim Abu Aziz), Eliza Dushku (Dana Tasker), Charlton Heston (Spencer Trilby), Mike Cameron (Citation Pilot)

Plot: Harry Tasker is a secret agent, so secret that even his family don't realise. However, a battle with terrorists means that he can no longer keep his secret life...

Inspiration: Emulating *Star Wars* creator George Lucas, James Cameron spent his time between projects creating his own special effects company which would work on his films as well as those of other directors. Along with long-time Cameron effects troubleshooter Stan Winston and former ILM president Scott Ross, the director founded Digital Domain. At the same time, Cameron's Lightstorm production company struck an exclusive deal with 20th Century-Fox that would unite the director and the studio for his future projects, including *True Lies* and *Titanic*.

During 1991 Cameron met with *Spider-Man* creator Stan Lee to discuss the character's movie possibilities. Along with pursuing *The Crowded Room* – even lining up John Cusack to play Multiple Personality Disorder patient Billy Milligan – Cameron was keeping his eyes on the tangled *Spider-Man* rights situation. Concluding it'd be another five years at least until the big screen rights were sorted out in the courts, Cameron began looking elsewhere for his next project.

One of Cameron's ideas was given away to his ex-wife, Kathryn Bigelow. Admitting that the marriage was over, the pair had quietly divorced on 30 August 1991. Citing "irreconcilable differences," Bigelow, at least, was willing to admit that their work had taken the place of their personal life: "There is always a price for doing what you want to do, and I guess that price for me was my marriage," she told *The Sunday Times*. The price for James Cameron in the divorce was the $1 million house they shared, which was handed over to Bigelow, and Cameron's commitment to produce three further films for Bigelow: the kind of trading of film industry credibility which substitutes for custody of the kids or financial penalties in Hollywood divorces. Faced with working through that three-picture debt to Bigelow, Cameron persuaded her to accept an idea he had for a film set around New Year's Eve 1999 concerning virtual reality, addiction, drugs and violence. The idea for *Strange Days* dated back almost a decade. Cameron had cooled on the notion of making the film himself, so he successfully palmed it off on his ex-wife. Cameron wrote the screenplay and served as executive producer, fulfilling his divorce settlement obligations.

A new idea had secured Cameron's interest: a 1990s James Bond-style movie, part thriller, part comedy. The opportunity to make *True Lies* came from Arnold Schwarzenegger. The actor had become aware of a 1991 French film called *La Totale!* (there's no indication that Arnie actually watched the subtitled French-language movie). It told the tale of a timid civil servant who hides from his unsuspecting wife that he's really a globe-trotting, terrorist-defying superspy. It seemed an ideal vehicle for Schwarzenegger to play both sides of his film personality (action man versus comedy, *Commando* versus *Twins*) and an opportunity for James Cameron to try something new: comedy. "I wanted to do a comedy, as well as a big action and visual picture," Cameron told *The Los Angeles Times*. "I knew it would be a challenge. Besides, the whole James Bond spy genre had not really aged well. I felt it was time to pump some new blood into it."

In the early 1990s the Bond franchise was deep in the doldrums. Timothy Dalton had brought a different kind of James Bond to life in his two hard-edged late-1980s outings – *The Living Daylights* (1987) and *Licence To Kill* (1989) – but they were not to everyone's tastes. It wouldn't be until 1995 – post-*True Lies* – that James Bond would really return in *Goldeneye*, with Pierce Brosnan playing the part. Cameron preferred to craft a knowing pastiche of the genre, rather than direct a genuine James Bond movie.

The original French movie was a low-key comedy-drama. Cameron knew that to turn *La Totale!* into a 'James Cameron movie' he'd need to pump up the source material considerably. Cameron called on Randy Frakes to beef up the drama. He also involved special effects supervisor John

Bruno (who'd worked on *The Abyss*) in devising affordable and achievable action set pieces.

Development: The casting of the lead character in *True Lies*, unlikely secret agent Harry Tasker, was a foregone conclusion. The fact that Arnold Schwarzenegger had brought the project to Cameron meant he'd be a sure thing for the leading role. As a result, Cameron found himself having to cast around his leading man. For the part of Helen, Tasker's unaware wife, Cameron settled on Jamie Lee Curtis, whom he'd met on the set of Bigelow's *Blue Steel*. Daughter of Tony Curtis and Janet Leigh, Jamie Lee Curtis had enjoyed a varied screen career from John Carpenter's *Halloween* (1978) through 1981's Eddie Murphy comedy *Trading Places* to *A Fish Called Wanda* (1988) and *Blue Steel*. Cameron needed an actress who could play homely, but also be sexy when required and cope with the stunts at the climax of *True Lies*.

For the role of Tasker's bumbling sidekick, Cameron took a leap and picked Tom Arnold, then best known for his stormy marriage to Roseanne Barr than for any significant acting achievements. Despite the unlikely casting choice, Arnold won the role of Gib while Cameron regular Bill Paxton – perhaps better suited to the sidekick role – played conman Simon.

Casting terrorist leader Aziz was a harder task. The director made a habit of always auditioning actors for a role, no matter who they were, but so taken was he by Art Malik's performance in the James Bond movie *The Living Daylight* (backed up with a viewing of *City Of Joy*) that Cameron offered Malik the role without an audition. Aware that the film was a big-budget comedy-thriller, Malik made the choice to play the part of Aziz as a straight role, which resulted in his character being out of kilter with the rest of the movie, as well as being a lightning rod for criticism.

With production backed by 20th Century-Fox as part of his new deal, Cameron set about filming *True Lies* with a budget of $70 million (upped by $10 million when Fox executives saw the finished script) and a 130-day shooting schedule. No sooner was Cameron back in action than the Hollywood trade press was on his case. Was the man who habitually made the world's most expensive movies going to do it again? Was the *True Lies* budget really more than $100 million, not the $70 million being admitted to? Was Cameron going to leave his wife for his leading lady once again?

In Spring 1992, Linda Hamilton gave birth to Cameron's daughter Josephine. The pair were not married and their relationship was not at its healthiest. Prior to starting shooting on *True Lies* Linda Hamilton moved out of the home she shared with Cameron, taking their daughter, Josephine, with her. Claiming this was not a separation, Cameron said: "We're both pretty happy with the arrangement..." Naturally, the press had a field day: Cameron was making another budget-busting movie, he was the subject of a lawsuit and his actress partner had left him, taking their daughter.

By July 1993, with filming on *True Lies* just weeks away, Cameron was the subject of legal action from his production partner on *The Crowded Room*, Sandra Arcara, and the real-life subject of the movie, Billy Milligan. Events came together on 3 August 1993. That was the first scheduled day of shooting on *True Lies*. It was also the day Cameron completed his first draft screenplay for *Spider-Man*. The same day saw Milligan drop his lawsuit. Six days later the director and Sandra Arcara came to an agreement: all the legal cases would be dropped, but Cameron would give up to Arcara all his rights to *The Crowded Room*. The deal allowed Cameron to forget about his abortive efforts on the MPD drama and concentrate on the task of bringing *True Lies* to the screen.

Production: Luckily for all concerned on the production of *True Lies*, the first few days of filming – which saw Cameron distracted by the resolution of *The Crowded Room* legal cases – concerned the domestic scenes between Harry and Helen Tasker. Nothing too elaborate or challenging there... It also gave all involved a false view that *True Lies* might be an easy, untroubled production. Obviously, those who thought that had also forgotten they were working for James Cameron.

With the easy stuff in the can, the production relocated to Miami, Florida, for the more elaborate flying and action sequences. For scenes featuring Arnold Schwarzenegger flying a Harrier jump jet through the cityscape of Miami, Cameron's original plan was to film the actor in a full-scale recreation of the jet in a studio against a blue screen. These scenes would then be integrated into background plates shot in the real location. John Bruno, however, suggested to Cameron that they build the motion control rig and the jet on top of a Miami building and shoot the sequence *in situ*.

On the first day of shooting with the rig in Miami in September 1993, Cameron opted to shoot one of the more complicated manoeuvres first, against the wish of rig operator Mark Noel, who wanted to wait a week or so before tackling the difficult scenes. With Schwarzenegger strapped into the cockpit, Cameron wanted the jet to execute a pitch-and-roll sequence while firing the guns. Problems with the rig, the Miami weather (extreme heat, unpredictable rainfall and unexpected rooftop lightning strikes) and the star (Cameron refused to allow Schwarzenegger to have a toilet break) all served to put the film behind schedule.

Cameron had scheduled three weeks for the filming of the rooftop jet scenes. He put in a request to 20th Century-Fox for more time and an increase in budget to allow him to capture the scenes he required. Already faced with overruns on the $70 million committed, Fox refused to allow any extra filming days or an increased budget. The director's Roger Corman film factory training quickly came into effect, as he opted to find a way to get the shots he needed. The result was that he actually saved a day on the rooftop filming schedule by shooting an action sequence with stuntmen on the jet at the same time as a crane was lifting the plane to remove the prop from the location. He'd avoided several set-ups and optical work in post-production, saving time and money.

The tyrant image had already stuck and the stories seemed to be confirmed when Cameron took to wielding a megaphone during the rooftop shooting in Miami. The megaphone soon became an entire bank of speakers which would broadcast Cameron's ravings to most of downtown Miami. Among the epithets he threw out were the phrases "That's exactly what I don't want!" and "Don't worry, I've worked with children before."

"I'm not a perfectionist," the director had claimed in *Premiere* magazine. "I only want to do it until it's great." Sometimes great wasn't good enough... An explanation for the switch in James Cameron's character emerged during the shooting of *True Lies*. How could he be charming, witty and great to work with one minute, then turn into an abusive, aggressive, obsessive madman the next? It was clear: there were two Jim Camerons: one called Jim by the crew, the other, evil incarnation dubbed 'Mij.' The idea of Mij, the dark side of Jim Cameron, the Hyde to Cameron's usual Jekyll, had surfaced among his film crews as early as *Aliens*. It was during *True Lies*, though, that the concept of Mij became so widespread, it got back to the director himself. "I don't like myself when I'm working," Cameron admitted in *Esquire*. "I'm like a machine. Day after day of shooting and I still feel like I'm failing..." Mij was the unstoppable Terminator movie director within mild-mannered Jim, the Kyle Reese who conceived the films.

True Lies climaxes with a ridiculously over-the-top helicopter and limousine chase along Florida's famous Seven Mile Bridge. The sequence took three weeks to shoot and a lot of post-production work to pull off. Jamie Lee Curtis, upon reading the script, assumed that a stuntwoman would play her role of Helen in this sequence (just as Ed Harris had assumed experienced stunt divers would cover for him on *The Abyss*). Her character was due to hang from a helicopter on a wire over 100 feet above the water. A few days before the scene was to be shot, Cameron approached Curtis and suggested she do the scene for real. "I asked if he'd be up there," Curtis told *Premiere*. "Jim said, 'I'll be shooting you.' I was hanging by this wire and Jim was acting as his own cameraman, hanging out the helicopter, filming the scene. It was like he wouldn't let me take the risk without taking it right along with me."

The filming of the climatic sequence came at a tough time for Cameron. Executives from 20th Century-Fox had been viewing the dailies from *True Lies*, and while praising the director for the images he was capturing on film, they were concerned about budgetary overruns. The budget was in danger of heading north of $100 million, with the 130-day shooting moving towards a 180-day epic. Pressure was put on Cameron to wrap as soon as he could, just when he was caught up in shooting one of the film's most dangerous sequences. On top of that, Cameron's relationship with Linda Hamilton was suffering and he wasn't being the new father he thought he could be. However, rather than let Mij loose again on the *True Lies* cast and crew, Cameron realised the end was in sight. Perhaps it was a sign of a new maturity in the director that rather than take his frustrations out on the cast and crew (which had been the case on *The Abyss*), Cameron knuckled under and finished the shooting as soon as he could.

When the film wrapped in March 1994, several of the cast were able to take stock of what they had been involved in. Bill Paxton had been with the project so long, he'd been able to go off and play the lead in another movie before returning to *True Lies*. Actress Tia Carrere characterised the production using a popular advertising slogan. "It just keeps going and going," she said of *True Lies*, "just like the Energizer bunny!" Fox executives let out a sigh of relief, then added up the cost: $120 million spent over seven months (Carrere had only signed on for seven weeks!)

Thinking the toughest part of this project was over, James Cameron was prepared to relax through post-production. Jumping between several editors toiling away in individual editing bays, just as he had on *Terminator 2*, Cameron supervised the first cut. To his horror, the director discovered he had some sequences that simply wouldn't cut together, the kind of elementary mistake that novice film-makers make... Cameron was quick to call on Arnold Schwarzenegger (who had moved on to begin lensing *Junior*) to shoot some extra coverage. Fox were none too happy to be hit with a further cost. To the press, Fox were denying the $120 million tag, but the story that James Cameron had just spent the most amount of money *ever* making a movie would not die.

July 1994 was set as the release date, but as it drew closer, *True Lies* was caught up in a public relations nightmare. The National Council of Islamic Affairs arranged a boycott of the movie for its alleged anti-Islam and anti-Arab tone. Women's groups also complained that Cameron's treatment of the Jamie Lee Curtis character (who is made to strip for her husband under duress) revealed a misogynistic streak. Cameron stayed silent on both topics, but faced with recovering its investment Fox added a special disclaimer to the film: 'This film is a work of fiction and does not represent the action or beliefs of a particular culture or religion.'

Reception: '141 minutes of an enticing three-minute trailer.' – *Daily Variety*. '*True Lies* delivers lots of ballistics for the buck. A loud misfire. It rarely brings its potent themes to life.' – *Time*. 'A strain of crudeness and mean-spirited humiliation runs through the film like a nasty virus.' – *The Los Angeles Times*. 'A furiously inventive thrill-packed movie. When a film-maker's idea of mind-boggling mayhem is this sensational, it's quite enough. It's the first successful romantic comedy in which trucks as well as heartstrings are blown to bits.' – *The New York Times*. '*True Lies* is a mess: bumpy, often stupid and crass.' – *New York Magazine*. 'Mind-boggling firepower and cartoony, over-the-top action.' – *Los Angeles Village Voice*. '*True Lies* is silly, spectacularly and knowingly so.' – *Newsweek*.

Box Office: With a $25.5 million opening weekend, *True Lies* failed to keep up at the box office with Disney's *The Lion King* and Tom Hanks-starrer *Forrest Gump*, taking around $145 million domestic US and an all-in total of $375 million worldwide. The film was only marginally profitable for 20th Century-Fox, which only held the US domestic distribution rights. As a result, Cameron signed over his 'back end' (payable once the film is in profit) participation points back over to the studio.

Awards: Oscar nominations: One (visual effects).

Analysis: An often loud, over-the-top and sometimes nasty pastiche of the James Bond formula, *True Lies* was James Cameron let off the leash, allowed to produce the film he wanted to see with little restraint being exercised by those in a position to do so. It's essentially the film which Mij made. It's often unkind to its characters, to specific groups like Arabs and women, while outstaying its welcome. Perhaps it was reflective of his state of mind as his relationship with Linda Hamilton collapsed around him? There's no doubt that the film is spectacular, but the spectacle doesn't serve the story (unlike in *Titanic*). Like *The Abyss*, *True Lies* is the kind of film that a 16-year-old would fantasise making. Indeed, Cameron had garnered a huge fanbase in the 16-21 age group since *The Terminator* and *Aliens*, and

True Lies is tailor-made for that age group. It's only with *Titanic* that Cameron managed to create a film with wider appeal which still employed the spectacle he was, by now, rightly renowned for.

Rep Company: It's the Terminator himself, as hero Harry Tasker, and Bill Paxton as conman Simon (behind a nasty moustache).

Trivia: The US Government supplied three Marine Harriers and their pilots for a fee of $100,736 (that's $2,410 per hour). Jamie Lee Curtis did her helicopter stunt work on her birthday. When Arnold Schwarzenegger is at the urinal, the song he whistles is 'Edelweiss,' a traditional Austrian song first made famous in *The Sound Of Music* (1965).

The Verdict: 3/5

Terminator 2: 3-D (1996)

"Most of the 3-D movies that I've seen have maybe two shots that are memorable for having great 3-D [and] neither was something slamming you in the face."

– James Cameron

AKA *T2: 3-D: Battle Across Time (1996)*

Crew: Directors: James Cameron, John Bruno, Stan Winston; Writers: Adam J Bezark, James Cameron, Gary Goddard; Producers: Chuck Kaminsky (producer), Jessica Huebner (associate producer), Andrew Millstein (executive producer); Original music: Brad Fiedel; Cinematography: Peter Anderson (3-D), Russell Carpenter (live action); Film Editing: Allen Cappuccilli, Shannon Leigh Olds; Production Design: John Muto

Cast: Arnold Schwarzenegger (The Terminator), Linda Hamilton (Sarah Connor), Robert Patrick (T-1000), Edward Furlong (John Connor), Earl Boen (Dr Peter Silberman) and revolving live cast

Plot: An attraction at the Universal Theme Park (installed in summer 1996), *T2:3-D* invites the audience to a presentation of future technology by the Cyberdyne Corporation; creators of the T-800 Terminators and future creator of Skynet. Halfway through the presentation, they are sabotaged (live) by Sarah and John Connor (played by lookalike actors), who inform the audience of the future destruction Cyberdyne will bring to the world. The audience is soon joined by the T-1000 as well as the T-800 on stage via motorcycle. The T-800 grabs John and exits the stage via a 3-D time portal, quickly pursued by the T-1000. From there it is all 3-D movie magic in which the T-800 and John Connor must defeat Skynet which is guarded by the powerful T-1M (T-One Million).

Inspiration: About to turn 40, James Cameron had no intention of giving up his big spending, high octane ways. "I was looking for something that would be the next big challenge," Cameron said of *Terminator 2: 3-D: Battle Across Time*, the unique film ride he developed.

The rest of 1994 saw Cameron attend to his corporate interests in Lightstorm Entertainment and Digital Domain. He'd been very pleased with the work Digital Domain had done on *True Lies* and wanted to ensure that, in the manner of George Lucas and ILM, he'd have a top flight effects facilities house tied to him which was also able to secure other work to make it economical.

Legal problems continued to dog Cameron, with Harlan Ellison (who'd been acknowledged as the author of the source material for *The Terminator*) coming back to haunt the director. It had come to the attention of Ellison that there was no credit or acknowledgement for his work in the recently re-issued video release of *The Terminator*. Having fought Cameron in the courts once for his due credit, Ellison was not about to rest on his laurels. Ellison claimed he'd been told that Cameron had personally insisted in removing the writer's credit from the videos, although it was an allegation he couldn't prove. For his part, Cameron had never been happy about having to credit Ellison on the film which had made his name in Hollywood. Ellison went on to win the case a second time, securing an estimated $400,000 pay-off.

The possibility of returning to the world of *The Terminator* was in Cameron's mind, and not just because of the second Harlan Ellison court case. He'd been asked several times about making *Terminator 3*. Feeling like the story he had to tell had been wrapped up in the first two movies, Cameron saw no reason to make *T3*. He was however intrigued by an invitation to get involved in a 12-minute film ride which would function as a semi-sequel to *Terminator 2: Judgment Day*.

Late in 1992, the idea of a unique film ride had been raised with producer Gary Goddard by Universal Pictures. Goddard was President of Landmark Entertainment, the company behind several successful Universal Theme Park movie-based rides, including *Ghostbusters, Jaws* and *King Kong* (dubbed 'Kongfrontation'). Goddard and his chief ride designer Adam Bezark watched *Terminator 2* repeatedly to identify the key components of the Terminator world and concept they'd have to recreate for the ride.

Development: Settling on a mix of dynamic 3-D film, live action stage show and show-stopping stunt work, Goddard and his team developed a plan for a unique attraction dubbed *Terminator 2: 3-D: Battle Across Time*. Aware of the project, James Cameron became involved with a strict set of criteria to preserve the integrity of his film. "My initial contribution was to sell Universal on the idea that we needed the actual cast [of *Terminator 2*] and not just a bunch of generic actors. They suggested that the Terminator have his face pretty much blown off, meaning it wouldn't matter if it was Arnold Schwarzenegger. I couldn't see how that would work."

Cameron set to work on his own script and storyboards for the 12-minute film, drawing on work already done by Goddard and Bezark but tying the whole thing much closer to his Terminator mythology. Additionally, Cameron saw *T2: 3-D* as an opportunity for Lightstorm Entertainment and Digital Domain to show what they could do beyond the world of theatrical movies.

Development on the ride, including the new technologies required to meld the on-screen 3-D action with the live action mayhem unleashed upon the audience, took over a year. Cameron persuaded Schwarzenegger, Linda Hamilton, Robert Patrick and Edward Furlong to return to their roles in his latest big-budget epic, a film that would cost $60 million for just 12 minutes. The go-ahead was given in March 1995 with filming set to begin in May.

Production: "We wanted to do something spectacular," said Cameron of his approach to *T2: 3-D*. "There is an enhanced sense of reality that comes from [shooting on] the high-resolution 65mm format, mixed with the illusion of depth offered by 3-D. Combine this with the live action stuff and it's really quite effective."

Cameron recruited Digital Domain's Stan Winston and John Bruno to handle the film sequence requiring robots and pyrotechnics, while Cameron concentrated on working with the returning actors. As producer and visual effects supervisor, Cameron appointed Chuck Kaminsky, the man who'd given the director his first paying job on *Battle Beyond The Stars* at Roger Corman's New World Pictures 15 years previously.

Filming the 3-D action was an arduous process. The camera rig featured five separate 3-D cameras, weighing almost 400 pounds each, mounted together to keep them in registration. Cameron, Winston and Bruno were faced with shooting sequences which had to match the future world battles seen in both previous *Terminator* movies, but this time the viewer was going on the ride with the characters. Intending to return to the Kaiser Steel

Mill in Fontana, California, which had been used in both *Terminator* movies, Cameron had to switch to filming in an open pit mine near Eagle Mountain when he discovered the plant had already been dismantled (the original reason for his limited shooting time at the location on *Terminator 2*). Additionally, Cameron had to capture all the live action material over a two week period in mid-May because this was the only time all the cast members would be available together.

Titanic (1997)

"I'm the king of the world!"

– James Cameron

Crew: Director/Writer: James Cameron; Producers: James Cameron (producer), Pamela Easley (associate producer), Al Giddings (co-producer), Grant Hill (co-producer), Jon Landau (producer), Sharon Mann (co-producer), Rae Sanchini (executive producer); Original music: James Horner; Cinematography: Russell Carpenter; Film Editing: Conrad Buff, James Cameron, Richard A Harris; Casting: Suzanne Crowley, Mali Finn, Gilly Poole; Production Design: Peter Lamont; Art Direction: Martin Laing, Bill Rea; Set Decoration: Michael Ford; Costume Design: Deborah L Scott

Cast: Leonardo DiCaprio (Jack Dawson), Kate Winslet (Rose DeWitt Bukater), Billy Zane (Caledon 'Cal' Hockley), Kathy Bates (Mrs Margaret 'Molly' Brown), Bill Paxton (Brock Lovett), Gloria Stuart (Rose Dawson Calvert/Old Rose), Frances Fisher (Ruth DeWitt Bukater), Bernard Hill (Captain Edward John Smith), Jonathan Hyde (Joseph Bruce Ismay), David Warner (Spicer Lovejoy), Suzy Amis (Lizzy Calvert), Jenette Goldstein (Irish Mother), Van Ling (Chinese Man), James Cameron (Cameo as Steerage Dancer, uncredited)

Plot: There's this unsinkable boat...

Inspiration: With *Spider-Man* still on legal hold and nothing else lined up, Cameron turned his attention to a long-cherished project: a film about the sinking of the Titanic. "The tragedy of Titanic has assumed an almost mythic quality in our collective imagination," claimed the director.

The possibility of James Cameron making a Titanic movie had been around for a long time. The biggest stumbling block in securing studio interest was that the inevitable end of the story – the boat sinks – would be known to all. For Cameron, this was a benefit not a negative: "If the characters can draw you into the story, the love story, then everything you know is coming, the inevitable horrors that you know await these people, make the movie all the more affecting and poignant because you know these feelings they are having have a short time to flourish."

James Cameron's interest in the Titanic went back to the discovery of the wreckage in 1985. The 'unsinkable' ocean liner hit an iceberg in the early hours of the morning of 15 April 1912, taking over an hour to actually sink beneath the waves. An expedition led by Dr Robert Ballard discovered the final resting place of the ship in 1985, broken in two, lying over 12,000 feet below sea level. Ballard had spent years on the project, developing special equipment to take him and his crew to the wreck. Similarly, Cameron would develop special camera equipment and techniques to recreate the ship and to allow him to visit and film the real wreckage. Cameron saw Ballard's footage from his remotely operated camera in the 1987 National Geographic Explorer documentary on the project. Having already made *The Abyss*, where he treated underwater like outer space, as envisaged in *Aliens*, Cameron felt his new 'underwater' movie would have to take a much more realistic approach.

Back in 1987, Cameron had written notes for a possible Titanic movie, reproduced in Paula Parisi's detailed account of the film's making, *Titanic And The Making Of James Cameron*. 'Do story with modern bookends of present-day scene of wreck using submersible, intercut with memories of survivor and recreated scenes of the night of the sinking. A crucible of human values under stress. A certainty of slowly impending doom. Divisions of men doomed and women and children saved by customs of the times. Many dramatic moments of separation, heroism and cowardice, civility versus animal aggression. Needs a mystery or driving plot element woven through...' There, in a nutshell in 1987, was James Cameron's *Titanic*.

Development: Cameron had a meeting with 20th Century-Fox executives to pitch his *Titanic* treatment. They had several reservations about the project. *Titanic* was a period piece, therefore a tough sell to modern, young audiences. The special effects requirements, which Cameron outlined when describing the hour of film time he'd take to show the boat sinking, recalled *True Lies*' budget busting $120 million cost. Additionally, filming in and around water was never easy or cheap, as Cameron himself had proved with *The Abyss*. Finally, after battling studios over the running times of his films *Aliens* and *The Abyss*, Cameron insisted that *Titanic* would be a three-hour epic.

There was only one way that Fox would take a chance on Jim Cameron and *Titanic*: they'd share the risk with another studio. Paramount Pictures was persuaded to join Fox in developing *Titanic*. In return for $60 million, Paramount would enjoy the distribution rights for the film within the US, while Fox would retain the rights to distribute the film overseas. In February 1995, James Cameron's *Titanic* was given a green light. Filming would begin in July 1996, with release set for one year later in July 1997.

Cameron and Fox knew they needed the right cast to hold an audience rapt to the cinema screen for three hours. Cameron wanted to shoot the film with no star names, and for good reason. "Who was 19 or 20 years old, a star and who filled my requirements? The answer was nobody," claimed Cameron. The pressure was on from Fox to cast a big name, and Cameron found himself having to fend off Tom Cruise, who expressed strong interest. "Cruise was too old," Cameron told *Movieline*. "I could have made *Titanic* as a Tom Cruise movie, but then I would have had to change the whole thing..."

Cameron's plot called for young, 19- or 20-year-old male and female leads, preferably not that well known. Working a class conflict into the doomed romance, Cameron created the character of third-class passenger Jack Dawson (who wins his ticket for the ship by gambling) and first-class passenger Rose DeWitt Bukater (named after Cameron's grandmother, Rose). "I hoped Rose and Jack's relationship would be a kind of emotional lightning rod, allowing viewers to invest their minds and their hearts, making history come alive again. Their connection on an emotional level is what transforms Rose from this sort of Edwardian geisha who is dying on the inside into this modern, spirited young woman on the cusp of a new life. Jack possesses this natural energy and purity of spirit which makes that transformation possible."

Casting Jack and Rose was difficult. Cameron needed young people up to the physical requirements of the film, as well as skilled actors who could carry the emotional weight of the drama. The first of the pair cast was 22-year-old British actress Kate Winslet. "I resisted Kate when she was initially suggested," Cameron admitted. He was aware she'd been Oscar-nominated for *Sense And Sensibility* (1995) and had seen the actress in Peter Jackson's *Heavenly Creatures* (1994). At the audition, Cameron thought Winslet too associated with historical films for her to work as the very modern Rose. "I thought, 'She does period movies, I don't want that.' I wanted to be able to take the audience through that barrier with someone new. I wanted somebody who could act as a conduit for our present-day emotions, who would be from that time and still be just like us." Among the actresses Cameron was considering for the role of Rose were Gwyneth Paltrow, *Romeo + Juliet*'s Clare Danes and French-born Gabrielle Anwar. However, Winslet's audition served to convince Cameron that the young actress was right for the role. "I realised she was just about the most talented actor around for her age. There was such a luminous quality in her face, voice and eyes that I knew audiences would be ready to go the distance with her..."

Cameron also had reservations about casting Leonardo DiCaprio as Jack, another suggestion from his casting director Mali Finn (she'd brought Winslet to Cameron's attention and had found Edward Furlong for *Terminator 2*). "Luck was a factor in casting Leo," admitted Cameron, who'd considered the actor for his version of *Spider-Man*. "I just felt you'd care about him a lot more. He has tremendous on-screen vitality. Leo has a wiry, survival quality about him..." However, DiCaprio himself proved to be reluctant to take the role. Cameron had only seen one film of DiCaprio's, *What's Eating Gilbert Grape?* (1993) which, like Winslet, had seen the actor nominated for an Oscar. Having decided on Winslet, Cameron arranged for her to act opposite DiCaprio during his audition. However, DiCaprio refused to allow the audition to be taped, so Cameron had nothing to show the studio executives. "Leo decided that he didn't want to do it," Cameron told *Movieline*. "He decided [Jack] wasn't quirky enough for him. I told him that wasn't the character, that Jack was like Jimmy Stewart, pure of heart. Then the light bulb went on for Leo and he realised it would be a really hard thing to make great. He really needed to be chased, to be seduced. He had misgivings about appearing in a big picture." As with Winslet, Cameron had been looking at other actors for the role, an important factor should DiCaprio spurn the part. Among those lined up as potential Jacks were Billy Crudup, while Fox were suggesting Cameron look at Chris O'Donnell or Matthew McConaughey. Feeling they were all too old for the part, Cameron continued to work on DiCaprio. "I always trust my first impression. It sounds corny, but that's what the audience does," Cameron told Paula Parisi. Finally a deal was closed in June, with Winslet signed on for $1 million and DiCaprio agreeing to $2.5 million, twice his usual fee following the remarkable success of *Romeo + Juliet*.

Production: Hiring Russian-owned submersible Mir vehicles, James Cameron set out in July 1996 to dive to the actual Titanic wreckage and film material to be used in the movie. Cameron had spent years in contact with the Russians to make his use of the subs possible, as well as years in development, with his brother Mike (through their Lightstorm Technologies company) to develop cameras and lenses which would make the filming possible.

The Halifax shoot was planned to last 10 days and featured Bill Paxton as modern-day treasure hunter Brock Lovett outlining his search for the valuable necklace, *le coeur de la mer*, lost when the Titanic sank. This was the 'mystery or driving plot element woven through...' that Cameron had realised in 1987 he'd need to hold the story together. Naturally, in true James Cameron style, this first part of the shoot went over time and over budget, taking 40 days and nights.

That was just the start of the trouble on *Titanic*. As well as the biggest and most expensive movie he'd ever made, *Titanic* was to be the film on which Cameron would suffer the worst press of his career. It's difficult to think back before *Titanic* became the biggest grossing film of all time, to before Cameron became the self-crowned 'King of the World,' to before the clean sweep of the Oscars. During the making of the film, *Titanic* was expected to be nothing less than a major turkey, and possibly the biggest flop of all time, not one of the most popular films of the 20th century.

Apart from the usual overruns and delays, complicated by shooting on water, the first section of production on *Titanic* was disrupted by a much more unusual and news-worthy act of sabotage. The final night of shooting in Nova Scotia on 8 August should have been like any other. Bill Paxton, who'd generally avoided the on-set food, sticking to hamburgers, decided to join the rest of the cast and crew in sampling the specially prepared wrap night clam chowder. Unfortunately, this chowder had an extra special ingredient: PCP or angel dust. Eighty members of the production, including Paxton and Cameron had to be taken to the Dartmouth General Hospital, where the true extent of the situation became apparent. "It's like total bedlam. People are coming on to this PCP, and there's all kinds of bizarre behaviour," recalled Paxton.

Once given the all clear, Paxton returned to his trailer but it took another 14 hours before he was feeling himself again. It was two weeks before an explanation for what had happened that night became clear after chemical analysis of the food. Rumours spread that two cooks fired the night before were responsible or, alternatively, it was one of the crew who'd finally had enough of working with James Cameron. "There were a lot of disgruntled people on that film," remembered Paxton. "Jim is not one of those guys who has the time to win the hearts and minds of the people. He is a driven, passionate, uncompromising, defiant, independent film-maker, artist and visionary. You gotta keep up with Jim; he's not going to keep up with you. I don't think they were ready for this guy..." The caterer who'd served the chowder, Earle Scott of Quality Foods, blamed the film-makers themselves. "It was that Hollywood crowd bringing all that psychedelic shit for their own amusement. I think it was a party that just got out of hand." Despite a police investigation by the Halifax force, sparked by rumours of on-set drug dealing, the case was quickly closed without a culprit or culprits ever being identified.

Returning to LA on 9 August, the *Titanic* circus was a week over schedule and way over budget. Panic set in among the executives of Fox and Paramount (a familiar feeling for them when working with James Cameron), aware that Cameron had not yet even shot on the expected-to-be-expensive *Titanic* set. With the budget at $110 million, Paramount capped their share at $65 million, forcing Fox to pick up any additional costs above that amount. To ensure he stayed in production, Cameron even signed over his own fee and profit participation, meaning he'd make no money from *Titanic*.

With Digital Domain ensconced in the old Hughes Aircraft hanger at Playa Vista in LA, Cameron and crew headed south to the newly-constructed Fox Baja studios in Mexico where a giant tank capable of holding a scaled replica of the Titanic had been constructed. While the guys from Digital Domain were building models, both physically and in computers, to match Cameron's deep dive Titanic footage, James Cameron was building the real thing at 90 per cent scale in the world's largest open air water tank.

By mid-September 1996, Kate Winslet and Leonardo DiCaprio were on set shooting scenes on the dominating Titanic ship set. Winslet didn't even have a chance to get used to her period costume as she wouldn't be wearing one for her debut scene, which involved Winslet's unabashed Rose stripping off to be sketched by DiCaprio's shy artist Jack. "It created a kind of tension and nervousness between them that served the scene very well," recalled Cameron. "I give them enough credit as actors that they could have created that [tension] even if it was the last day of the shoot, but I think the fact that it worked out that way actually gave the scene a certain tangible something..."

Each accident among the crew building the Titanic replica at the Rosarito Beach location had been reported gleefully in the press. Eight people had been injured, with one requiring surgery to remove a damaged spleen. The press reckoned it was only a matter of time until one of the prominent actors involved in the project was injured too.

The struggle to capture the reality of life on board the Titanic, both before and during the sinking, took its toll on the cast and crew. Wound up by his slipping schedule and escalating costs, Cameron's mask quickly slipped and evil alter ego Mij was let loose. Extras and technicians were verbally abused and fired. DiCaprio was quietly told never to be late to Cameron's set again, and such was the menace in the director's tone the actor turned up on time, every time. For the most part, Winslet and DiCaprio avoided the wrath of Mij which, as often before, seemed to be mostly reserved for his crew rather than his cast. "Jim has a temper like you wouldn't believe," a stunned Kate Winslet told *The Los Angeles Times*. "I think the actors got off lightly. Jim knew he couldn't shout at us the way he did to his crew because our performances would be no good."

The injury to a star that the press had been waiting for came when DiCaprio took a tumble running through a crowd along a wet gangplank in a scene ultimately not used in the film. Falling to the deck, DiCaprio tumbled under the legs of a horse. Cameron judged his star unhurt and quickly called for another take. Similarly, Winslet suffered various minor injuries. "It was an ordeal," she recalled in *The Los Angeles Times*. "I chipped a small bone in my elbow. I had deep bruises all over my arms. I looked like a battered wife! I slipped on the deck at one point and I got an ugly gash on my knee..."

Time magazine reported in December 1996 that extras were rushed to a local hospital with broken ribs and sprained ankles. The shooting of the climatic sinking scenes of the movie also took their toll. The 750ft long replica of the ship was rigged to split in two and be tipped up by hydraulics. Ten crew members ended up having to undergo surgery of one sort or another after falling on railings during these scenes. Eight weeks into shooting and problems had developed with Cameron's giant *Titanic* set - the hinges holding the two parts of the giant boat together broke rather than bending, plummeting part of the expensive set 47 feet to the water below. Such was the concern for the health and safety of those making *Titanic* that the Screen Actors Guild sent a representative to monitor the production.

Following the strife on the set, the next favourite topic of the Hollywood press when it came to *Titanic* was the budget. First it was $110 million, then $120 million... With neither Paramount nor Fox willing to confirm a figure during production, speculation ran riot. Was it $150 million? $180 million? Whatever, *Titanic* was now officially regarded as the most expensive motion picture ever made, and it was only halfway through shooting. At these kinds of costs, if the movie failed at the box office, there was a good chance that one or both of the studios financing it would be destroyed in its wake. It had happened before in Hollywood with *Heaven's Gate* (1980).

Personally, the toll was beginning to tell on the director. Separated from Linda Hamilton during filming (she was off making volcano movie *Dante's Peak*), Cameron had become involved with actress Suzy Amis, cast as Rose's granddaughter in the contemporary scenes shot in Halifax. When Amis turned up on the Mexican set (even though her character naturally could not be in the 1912-set sequences), the press had a field day. In an attempt to salvage things, Hamilton flew to Mexico to spend time with Cameron. Connoisseurs of the tales of Mij enjoyed hearing about the time when Cameron supposedly grabbed a rifle and began shooting at extras in the water who refused to drown on cue. Although that incident apparently didn't happen, many others did and several extras came down with hypothermia as a result of spending far too long immersed in freezing cold water while Cameron insisted on getting the 'right' shots for his film.

Concern, mainly fuelled by press reports, grew within 20th Century-Fox, so much so that in November 1996 Fox Chairman Bill Mechanic decided to make a personal visit to the *Titanic* location. The main subject discussed at the meeting at Rosarito Beach between Mechanic and Cameron was *Titanic*'s swelling budget. Here Cameron was repeating a pattern that had become all too familiar. Mechanic had brought with him an annotated script, suggesting scenes which could be cut to save money. This did not go down well with Cameron. Reports from the meeting suggest that Cameron lost his cool, storming out leaving Mechanic with the impression that his director had just quit the film. "It was my lowest point," admitted the executive. "He told me where to go and walked off..."

Titanic had been filming for five months and was upwards of $50 million over budget. Mechanic's concerns seemed reasonable, but that wasn't how James Cameron saw it. Having seen off what he perceived as interference from the studio, he set about reasserting his authority on the *Titanic* set. At 42, Cameron realised he was too old for throwing tantrums and storming off sets, even if the press didn't. Besides, his career would never recover if the director were to quit the biggest budgeted film in history without finishing it...

Cameron was cheered when in January 1997 the Screen Actors Guild investigation into safety on the *Titanic* set was published, giving the production a clean bill of health. "Not only did SAG find zero proof to support the allegations reported in the press," claimed Ken Orsatti, SAG national executive director, "it concluded that the producers may have set a new standard in pre-production spending for the sole purpose of medical emergency planning." The good ship *Titanic* was back on an even keel.

The last scenes of the 210-day shoot were captured in March 1997, as DiCaprio and Winslet played out their final scenes in the water. It was Kate Winslet rather than James Cameron who called a halt to the filming. Having endured hours in the water, weighted down and struggling to breathe using a concealed air regulator, the actress declared she'd run out of patience. "After three takes I simply said I couldn't do any more," she admitted. That left James Cameron with little choice but to declare a wrap.

The project was far from finished, and although the intense day-to-day work with actors under extremely trying conditions was at an end, Cameron had much still to do in post-production to bring his vision to fruition. By April, Cameron was directing the special effects crew at Digital Domain in southern California, rather than actors in a water tank in Mexico. However, the schedule-driven tensions were just the same.

Model-makers, cameramen, computer graphics animators and editors were all hard at work completing shots and creating elements to tie together the live action material. Working long hours under extreme pressure, mistakes were made. Some very expensive CGI work was discovered to have depicted the Titanic sailing in the wrong direction, resulting in some hasty remedial work. "There was such a lot of pressure being brought by Cameron," claimed one model-maker, "that there was a lot of panic."

With the July 1997 release date looming, James Cameron had to admit defeat. Retaking special effects sequences and his endless tinkering with the edit of the film meant that it simply wouldn't be ready to release on time. A three-and-a-half-hour version of the movie existed and had been screened to Fox executives, but everyone knew that the film could not be released at that length. The opening was moved to 19 December, sparking a flurry of media speculation that the film was in terrible trouble: as well as being the most expensive movie ever made *Titanic* was doomed to become Hollywood's biggest ever flop.

Cameron's private life was back in the press, too, as he moved out of the house he shared with Linda Hamilton in April 1997 and began openly dating *Titanic* actress Suzy Amis. Cameron suddenly developed a hankering for domestic stability. With *Titanic* seemingly falling apart around him, he clung to the one certain thing he had in his life: his family. Hamilton gave Cameron an ultimatum: a sure sign of his commitment and an end to his affair with Amis or the end of their relationship. The result was a hasty marriage in July 1997 as Linda Hamilton became the third Mrs Cameron.

Back at work, Cameron edited *Titanic* down to three hours and 14 minutes, refusing to trim the film any further. With the almost 200 special effects shots just about completed, it looked like the film would make its second release date and a world premiere in Japan with time to spare. "It was gruelling and taxing and all that stuff," said Cameron of his *Titanic* experience, "but the hardest thing to do on this film was to focus on what was going on in terms of the human heart of the film. If you blow that, then all that other stuff doesn't mean anything." It appeared that in the process of shooting *Titanic*, James Cameron had matured in many ways, as a man and as a film-maker.

Reception: '*Titanic* is the first spectacle in decades that honestly invites comparison to *Gone With The Wind*. A huge, thrilling three-and-a-quarter-hour experience that unerringly lures viewers into the beauty and heartbreak of its lost world.' *–The New York Times.* 'The allure of *Titanic* is in its invitation to swoon at a scale of epic movie-making that is all but obsolete.' – *Newsweek.* '*Titanic* is magnificent. An overwhelming visual, aural and emotional experience.' – *The New York Daily News*. 'The film is a daunting blend of state-of-the-art special effects melded around a sterling central story.' – *The Hollywood Reporter*. 'A spectacular demonstration of what modern technology can contribute to dramatic storytelling.' – *Variety*. 'The film can carry you away with sweet romance or leave you agog at majestic images... it can also leave you a giggle at ridiculous nonsense which would sink lesser vessels.' – *Wall Street Journal*. 'Seeing *Titanic* makes you want to weep in frustration. What really brings on the tears is Cameron's insistence that writing this kind of movie is within his abilities. Not only isn't it, it isn't even close.' – *The Los Angeles Times*. '[*Titanic* features] dramatic crudity, profoundly rotten dialogue, rough patches of Saturday morning animation... [yet] everyone feels they are obliged to like it.' – *Film Comment*.

Box Office: Titanic enjoyed the longest and most prosperous run at the worldwide box office of any film to date [2002]. The US opening weekend take of $29 million was followed by a second week's takings of a further $34 million, the reverse of most movie openings where box-office takings fall in subsequent weeks. Within 11 weeks total US takings were $402 million. By June 1998 *Titanic* topped $600 million at the domestic US box office, making the film the biggest earning movie of all time by some way. Overseas income boosted the total figure to over $900 million, easily covering the estimated below-the-line (before prints and advertising) cost of $200 million.

Awards: Oscars won: 11 (picture, director, cinematography, film editing, art direction, visual effects, sound, sound effects editing, song, score, costume); Oscar nominations: 14 (picture, director, actress, supporting actress, cinematography, film editing, art direction, visual effects, sound, sound effects editing, song, score, costume, make-up); With 14 Academy Award nominations, *Titanic* was not going to be leaving the 1998 Oscar ceremony empty-handed. The result was a record-breaking 11 Oscars, including Best Picture and Best Director Awards for James Cameron personally. Cameron was never going to be a shy and humble recipient of these awards: the pinnacle of achievement in Hollywood. With his infamous "I'm the king of the world" cry and his obsequious request for a moments silence to remember those who drowned on the ship, Cameron both claimed his Hollywood crown and made a fool of himself simultaneously. Was Mij in residence that night or was this a unjustly ignored American film-maker finally being given his due?

Rep Company: Returning from *Aliens* and *T2* is Jenette Goldstein as one of the upper-class matrons, while Bill Paxton turns up in the more substantial role of treasure hunter (and James Cameron alter ego) Brock Lovett.

Analysis: With *Titanic*, James Cameron finally managed to meld his high-tech flamboyant high-concept action movie sensibility with a human story, one with the potential to captivate and even move audiences. That's why *Titanic* worked: the repeat viewings at the cinema by teenagers (fans of DiCaprio and, to a lesser extent, Winslet) and older (over 50) cinema-goers ensured it would be the highest grossing film of all time. Cameron's script is, admittedly, no great shakes. Cameron has admitted on several occasions that screenwriting is not his strong point: he's a visual director. Some of the plotting is ropy, characterisation is basic and the dialogue is laughable in some places, but there was enough there in *Titanic* to capture and carry an audience along with the adventure. Cameron's obsession with dramatic visuals is finally put at the service of a very intimate personal story and this time it works (much more so than in *The Terminator* or *The Abyss*, where he tried to pull off the same trick). In fact, it can be argued that *Titanic* is the ultimate culmination of the James Cameron style of film-making... and that might be why he's been having such difficulty trying to decide what film to make next...

Trivia: As is the case with many 20th Century-Fox films, the film cans for the advance screening prints and show prints had a code name. *Titanic* was code-named *Baby's Day Out 2*. Before announcing development of *Titanic*, Cameron shot footage of icebergs off Nova Scotia under the cover of making a film called *Planet Ice*. The name of the character Caledon 'Cal' Hockley derives from two small towns (Caledon and Hockley) near Orangeville, Ontario, Canada, where Cameron's aunt and uncle live. Jack's sketch of Rose wearing the necklace was drawn by Cameron; it's his hands seen drawing the picture. Cameron also drew all the other pictures in Jack's sketchbook. Cameron was hesitant about including any song in the movie, even over the closing credits. Composer James Horner secretly arranged with lyricist Will Jennings and singer Céline Dion to write 'My Heart Will Go On' and record a demo tape, which he then presented to Cameron. The song went on to win an Oscar. At $200 million, the movie cost more than the Titanic itself. The cost to construct the ship in 1910-1912 was £1.5 million, equivalent to $7.5 million at the time and about $120 to $150 million in 1997 dollars.

The Verdict: 3/5

Dark Angel (TV series, 2000-2002)

"There's an energy to television. It keeps the creative wheels turning. For a perfectionist like me it takes away the need for perfection."

– James Cameron

Crew: Created by James Cameron and Charles H Eglee; Directors: David Nutter (pilot), Duane Clark, Sarah Pia Anderson, James A Contner, Joe Ann Fogle, David Jackson, Michael Katleman, Jefery Levy, Chris Long, Terrence O'Hara, Paul Shapiro, Jeff Woolnough among others; Writers: James Cameron & Charles H Eglee (pilot), Jose Molina (staff writer), Moira Dekker, René Echevarria, Doris Egan, Charles H Eglee, Patrick Harbinson, David Simkins, David Zabel among others; Producers: James Cameron (executive producer), René Echevarria (co-executive producer), Charles H Eglee (executive producer), Patrick Harbinson (supervising producer), Gina Lamar (associate producer), Rae Sanchini (co-executive producer); Original music: Chuck D & Gary G-Wiz (main theme), Joel McNeely; Cinematography: Peter Wunstorf; Film Editing: Stephen Mark; Casting: Eric Dawson, Carol Kritzer, Robert J Ulrich

Cast: Jessica Alba (Max Guevara/X-5 452), Michael Weatherly (Logan Cale/Eyes Only), Valarie Rae Miller (Cynthia 'Original Cindy' McEachin), William Gregory Lee (Zack/X-5 599), JC MacKenzie (Reagan 'Ray'/'Normal' Ronald), Jensen Ackles (Ben/Alec), Ashley Scott (Asha Barlow),

Kevin Durand (Joshua), Richard Gunn (Sketchy), Alimi Ballard (Herbal Thought), John Savage (Colonel Donald Lydecker), Nana Visitor (Dr Elizabeth Renfro/Madame X) Jennifer Blanc (Kendra Maibaum)

Plot: In a post-apocalyptic Seattle 20 years in the future, genetically engineered heroine Max (Jessica Alba) gets involved with 'Eyes Only,' subversive video broadcaster Logan Cale (Michael Weatherly).

Inspiration: Although he'd been paid $1.25 million to write the *Titanic* screenplay, by the time he collected his Oscar for Best Picture, James Cameron was running low on funds. Having signed away his directing fee and back-end participation on the film to ensure it got completed, he'd essentially been working on the movie for free for three years. Now the film was a phenomenal success, Fox (with the agreement of Paramount) decided to reinstate Cameron's back-end participation, paying him in the region of $100 million in April 1998.

On the personal front, things were once more difficult for Cameron. His all-or-nothing marriage to Linda Hamilton had hit a rocky patch and he was again seeing Suzy Amis. Cameron once again split with Hamilton, but the inevitable divorce settlement was complicated by the director's new-found wealth. Taking time away from film-making in the wake of *Titanic*'s unprecedented success, Cameron enjoyed diving and travelling. However, the urge to embark on another project was hard to resist.

James Cameron found his attention turning to television at the end of the 1990s. Fascinated by the prospect of exploring Mars, Cameron had toyed with turning Kim Stanley Robinson's trio of Mars novels (*Red Mars, Green Mars, Blue Mars*) into a TV mini-series. However, 20th Century-Fox television instead offered a 13-episode commitment to *Dark Angel*, about a genetically engineered heroine in the near future.

Linda Hamilton filed for divorce from James Cameron in December 1998, seeking custody of their five-year-old daughter, Josephine. By mid-1999 the divorce was final with Hamilton enjoying a large financial settlement, estimated by some media sources to be as high as $100 million. Cameron, meanwhile, purchased a new $4.4 million home in Santa Barbara, California.

Production/Reception: The first big challenge in switching from movies to television for James Cameron was coming to terms with television-sized budgets. "I'll admit that it's definitely a learning curve for me. It really reminds me of my roots as a guerrilla film-maker," said Cameron as he began work on *Dark Angel*'s debut season. Cameron hoped for a more forgiving environment on television where he'd have time to build an audience for his show across a period of time. "You can bring it out and start to create some good will with an audience. There's a freedom to roll with the punches." Cameron also saw his TV show as a return to the female action heroics of *Aliens* and *Terminator 2*. "Men are not put off by strong women in films," he said. "They want to see girls kick ass, too."

The first season had a slow start, failing to capture a large audience or a dedicated cult following. However, as the first series built to a shocking final episode, *Dark Angel* had gathered a strong international fanbase, but not stellar ratings.

Entering its second series on Fox during the 2001-2002 season, there were significant changes to *Dark Angel*. In addition to moving to a new 8pm Friday time slot, the show broadened its story beyond its genetically-enhanced heroine, Max. "What we want to do is expand the *Dark Angel* universe slightly," series co-creator James Cameron claimed. He described the changes as "turbocharging" the science fiction elements, playing up a theme of "biopunk" and introducing a host of new, genetically-altered characters called "trans-humans." Prime among these characters was Joshua, a dog-faced man played by Kevin Durand.

According to Cameron, the series heroine Max is "part of a persecuted minority, very self-conscious about people finding out who and what she is. She has to guard her secret even more closely. [That's] a microcosm for anybody that feels persecuted or alienated or misjudged in society," Cameron said.

Low ratings and the new Friday night time slot seemed to threaten the future of *Dark Angel* as the show entered the February sweeps period of 2002. Despite the addition of new characters and development of old characters, the time slot and a lack of serious promotion by Fox suggested that the future of the show might be short-lived. James Cameron's side trip to television seemed to be coming to an end.

As always, though, he had one final surprise up his sleeve. In an effort to push the show through to renewal for a third season, Cameron himself agreed to direct the season finale of the second year. "I believe in our show," said Cameron. "I think it is one of the coolest things on network television. I have wanted to direct an episode for some time, so when our director for the season finale dropped out just as I was completing photography on another project, I seized the moment."

Shooting the series finale for *Dark Angel*, Cameron stuck to tradition by coming in over-budget and over-schedule. The 90-minute episode 'Freak Nation' cost $3 million according to Cameron or around $10 million if sources at Fox are to be believed. Cameron claimed that if 90 minutes of TV cost $3 million, "theoretically I should be able to make a two-hour movie for about $5.5 million! I think some of the lessons I learned will be valuable from a film-making standpoint." Despite his personal involvement in making the last episode, Cameron's first attempt at a on-going TV series was cancelled after two years. *Dark Angel*'s demise appeared to have been engineered by Fox to make way for a new space show called *Firefly* from *Buffy The Vampire Slayer* creator Joss Whedon. Fox chief Gail Berman claimed the decision to can the series had been difficult: "It was a show which we liked and whose creators we admired. We felt in the end that we would go with some new programming..." For his part, Cameron was sanguine about the turn of events. "I think these decisions are made on a very mercenary basis. Once they've decided that they've got to put their money elsewhere, they'll put their money elsewhere. It's too bad, because I think we have a loyal fanbase." A fan driven letter writing campaign seemed unlikely to revive *Dark Angel*, even as a series of TV movies. "I doubt it, quite frankly," said Cameron.

6. Battle Across Time:
James Cameron's Future

"The future is unknowable. The only thing we truly own is today."

– James Cameron

Following the success of *Titanic*, the self-styled "King of the World" seemed at a loss as to what to do next. His diversion into television - developing the Mars Trilogy and creating *Dark Angel* - was little more than treading water.

Having achieved the pinnacle of his career with *Titanic*, Cameron found himself returning to the sea for the documentary film *Ghosts Of The Abyss*. The 45-minute film covers both the sinking of the Titanic and the German warship the Bismarck. At the time of shooting, Cameron said: "We have been preparing for this expedition for three years, putting together the technology to go beyond what's been done before. We have a very good team, many of whom were with me on the Titanic expedition." Joining Cameron on the project was his brother John David Cameron. The film-makers also used cameras and technology developed by Cameron's other brother Mike, who'd worked on both *The Abyss* and *Titanic*. Returning to past glories, though, didn't see Cameron moving forward with future film projects.

Among the films he considered was *True Lies 2* and *Terminator 3*. "I have a better idea for a second *True Lies* than I do for a third *Terminator*..." Cameron had always resisted the idea of a third *Terminator* movie, believing the story to be complete across the two movies he has made. That wouldn't stop others developing the films.

His script treatment for *Spider-Man* had moved that project forward and with the rights issue resolved by the courts in August 1998, it looked likely at one stage that the film would happen with Cameron helming and Leonardo DiCaprio starring. Instead, the film was eventually made in 2001 and released in spring 2002 with Tobey Maguire in the lead and Sam Raimi behind the camera. Cameron did, however, receive an on-screen credit for his development work on the project.

Planet Of The Apes, a remake of the ground-breaking 1968 SF classic, was another possible Cameron project due to reunite him with his *Terminator* and *True Lies* star Arnold Schwarzenegger. That one, too, slipped away from the director, passing instead to Tim Burton and proving to be one of the more disappointing films of 2001.

A much talked-about project called *Avatar*, about artificial life forms, and featuring six completely computer-generated characters, had been greenlit in 1997 but put on hold when it was realised that the budget required by the film would dwarf even that of *Titanic*. Development work on the characters had been done by Digital Domain. Cameron's idea for an asteroid disaster movie *Bright Angel Falling* fell by the wayside due to other asteroid movies in 1998. Through Lightstorm Cameron also bought the rights to an Anne Rice Mummy novel *Ramses the Damned* and the remake rights to the cerebral 1972 Russian SF movie *Solaris*. Only the latter was made, with Cameron producing and *Traffic*'s Steven Soderbergh directing.

Unable to settle on a project, the end of 2001 saw the director turning to comic books for inspiration. Lightstorm Entertainment contracted to develop and produce a live-action version of the Top Cow comic *Fathom*. Created by Michael Turner, it follows the adventures of a young woman found aboard an abandoned yacht. She becomes a champion swimmer and marine biologist but gradually discovers she possesses super powers. Cameron seems to have found a way of combining the female superheroics of *Dark Angel* with the underwater drama of *The Abyss* and *Titanic*. The rights had initially been purchased by Fox Animation two years previously, but when the studio cut back on animated projects, Fox brought it to Cameron as a feature project.

Whether *Fathom* comes to fruition or not, there will be some James Cameron material in cinemas in the early years of the 21st Century, even if he is not directly involved. The rights to the *Terminator* sequels have been revived and work on two new films proceeds without either Cameron or Schwarzenegger's involvement. It also seems likely that the part of John Connor would be recast, because the new producers don't want actor Edward Furlong involved. New characters, possibly including a female Terminator, are to be developed.

Cameron's personal life has also moved on. He married Suzy Amis in the summer of 2000 and she gave birth to Cameron's second child in May 2001. Having got through almost as many wives as films with almost as much *Sturm und Drang*, Cameron looks like he's finally settled down.

The problem for James Cameron is that he can no longer top himself. As each film he made became dubbed "the most expensive movie ever made" and a possible box-office turkey, he proved the critics wrong with acclaim, awards and box-office success for *Aliens, The Abyss, Terminator 2* and *Titanic*. Even his one bombastic failure, *True Lies*, has made its money back through VHS and DVD releases and has its fans. Having produced the most expensive movie and the world's biggest box-office success in *Titanic*, Cameron has nowhere to go in the world of film-making. It's almost inevitable that the next commercial mainstream movie he produces will be judged a failure when it doesn't replicate the box-office success of *Titanic*. His solution is the diversion into television with *Dark Angel,* continual technological experimentation and documentary making with *Ghosts Of The Abyss*. Eventually, though, he'll return to the director's chair. His fans will be waiting... as will the critics.

7. Resource Materials

Filmography

Ghosts Of The Abyss (producer, director, 2002)
Dark Angel (TV series, co-creator, executive producer, 2000-2002)
Titanic (director, writer, 1997)
T2: 3-D: Battle Across Time (theme park attraction, director, 1996)
Strange Days (producer, writer, 1995)
True Lies (producer, director, writer, 1994)
Terminator 2: Judgment Day (producer, director, writer, 1991)
Point Break (executive producer, uncredited rewrite, 1991)
The Abyss (director, writer, 1989)
Alien Nation (uncredited rewrite, 1988)
Aliens (director, writer, 1986)
Rambo: First Blood Part II (co-writer, 1985)
The Terminator (director, writer, 1984)
Android (design consultant, 1982)
Piranha 2: The Spawning (director, 1981)
Galaxy Of Terror (production designer, 1981)
Escape From New York (F/X director, 1981)
Battle Beyond The Stars (art director, 1980)

Books

Dreaming Aloud: The Life And Films Of James Cameron (1998) Christopher Heard, Doubleday
Titanic And The Making Of James Cameron (1998) Paula Parisi, Orion
James Cameron: An Unauthorized Biography (2000) Mark Shapiro, Renaissance Books
BFI Modern Classics: The Terminator (1996) Sean French, British Film Institute
BFI Modern Classics: Titanic (1999) David M Lubin, British Film Institute
James Cameron's Titanic (1997) Douglas Kirkland, Harper Collins
Ken Marschall's Art Of Titanic (1998) Ken Marschall, Hyperion

Articles

Fangoria 41, January 1985
Filmex 1985 Reader, March 15 1985
Orange County Register, July 13 1986
Washington Post, July 20 1986
Village Voice, July 22 1986
Fangoria 56, August 1986
People, August 11 1986
Hollywood Reporter 56th Anniversary Issue, November 24 1986
Movieline, August 11 1989
US, August 1991
Entertainment Weekly, August 30 1991
Hollywood Reporter, April 20 1993
Premiere, August 1994
Variety, February 24 1995
Hollywood Reporter (James Cameron Issue), March 7 1995
Box Office, October 1995
Hollywood Reporter, November 22 1995
Los Angeles Times Magazine, March 24 1996

Websites

Internet Movie Database: http://us.imdb.com/Name?Cameron,+James
James Cameron Links List: http://www.cogeco.ca/~ryanvb/links.htm
Unofficial James Cameron Website: http://come.to/JamesCameron
Terminator/Terminator 2/Terminator 2: 3-D Frequently Asked Questions:
   http://www.geocities.com/Hollywood/6601/page/faqlist/tfaq0.html

The Essential Library: Currently Available

Film Directors:

Woody Allen (2nd)	**Tim Burton**	**Ang Lee**
Jane Campion*	**John Carpenter**	**Joel & Ethan Coen (2nd)**
Jackie Chan	**Steve Soderbergh**	**Clint Eastwood**
David Cronenberg	**Terry Gilliam***	**Michael Mann**
Alfred Hitchcock (2nd)	**Krzysztof Kieslowski***	**Roman Polanski**
Stanley Kubrick (2nd)	**Sergio Leone**	**Oliver Stone**
David Lynch	**Brian De Palma***	**George Lucas**
Sam Peckinpah*	**Ridley Scott (2nd)**	**James Cameron**
Orson Welles (2nd)	**Billy Wilder**	
Steven Spielberg	**Mike Hodges**	

Film Genres:

Blaxploitation Films	**Bollywood**	**French New Wave**
Horror Films	**Spaghetti Westerns**	**Vietnam War Movies**
Vampire Films*	**Heroic Bloodshed***	
Slasher Movies	**Film Noir**	

Film Subjects:

Laurel & Hardy	**Marx Brothers**	**Film Music**
Steve McQueen*	**Marilyn Monroe**	**The Oscars®**
Filming On A Microbudget	**Bruce Lee**	**Writing A Screenplay**

TV:

Doctor Who

Literature:

Cyberpunk	**Philip K Dick**	**The Beat Generation**
Agatha Christie	**Sherlock Holmes**	**Noir Fiction***
Terry Pratchett	**Hitchhiker's Guide (2nd)**	**Alan Moore**

Ideas:

Conspiracy Theories	**Nietzsche**	**UFOs**
Feminism	**Freud & Psychoanalysis**	**Bisexuality**

History:

Alchemy & Alchemists	**The Crusades**	**The Black Death**
Jack The Ripper	**The Rise Of New Labour**	**Ancient Greece**
American Civil War	**American Indian Wars**	

Miscellaneous:

The Madchester Scene	**Stock Market Essentials**	**Beastie Boys**
How To Succeed As A Sports Agent		

Available at all good bookstores or send a cheque (payable to 'Oldcastle Books') to: **Pocket Essentials (Dept JCAM), 18 Coleswood Rd, Harpenden, Herts, AL5 1EQ, UK**. £3.99 each (£2.99 if marked with an *****) . For each book add 50p postage & packing in the UK and £1 elsewhere.